Swimming Against the Stream

SWIMMING AGAINST THE STREAM

Jean Perraton

With a foreword by Marion Shoard

Second revised edition

JON CARPENTER

Our books may be ordered from bookshops or (post free) from
Jon Carpenter Publishing, 19 The Green, Charlbury,
England OX7 3QA

First published in 2005 in this digital edition by
Jon Carpenter Publishing
19 The Green, Charlbury, Oxfordshire OX7 3QA
Tel 01608 819117

Second revised edition 2013

ISBN 978 1 906067 12 0

In memory of my mother and father who also enjoyed swimming

Contents

List of boxes   vi
List of tables   vii
List of illustrations   vii
Acknowledgements   viii
Foreword by Marion Shoard   x
Preface to the new edition   xiii
Introduction   xiv
Chapter 1: The summer's sovereign good   1
Chapter 2: A quick dip into the history of swimming   12
Chapter 3: Lost opportunities and continuing constraints   23
Chapter 4: The guardians of the water environment   33
Chapter 5: A countryside for all?   43
Chapter 6: Litigation or liberty?   53
Chapter 7: The cost of a quick dip – the danger of drowning   61
Chapter 8: The cost of a quick dip – the health hazards   70
Chapter 9: Who wants to swim?   79
Chapter 10: To cool in the dog days – health and happiness   88
Chapter 11: Tread lightly, swim gently – swimming and the environment   95
Chapter 12: Let's go out to swim – making it possible   102
Postscript   118
Notes   123
References   131
Index   140

List of boxes
A bath in Regent's Canal   17
A river for town and gown   20
Land of lost rivers and meres   25
A long swimming river   29
A jewel in the Welsh hills   46
No more bathing at Black Park   51
Caring council or corporate vandal?   57
A swim before work?   59
No swimming now in the New Sea   73

A city oasis – Henleaze Swimming Club   83
Rescuing Hatchmere Lake   85
Dubs and tarns in the Lake District   92
A lovely sandy beach for kids   104
Bathing is permitted here – but who knows?   113

List of tables

Table 4.1: Environment Agency: budget for recreation-related activities
    2004/05 (£m)   34
Table 4.2: British Waterways: income 2002/04 (£m)   37
Table 4.3: Bathing waters identified under the Bathing Water Directive, 1980   40
Table 4.4: Inland Bathing Waters in England and Wales: compliance with the
    Bathing Water Directive   41
Table 5.1: Water-based activities in country parks in England, 2002   50
Table 7.1: Activities associated with accidental drownings in the UK   62
Table 7.2: Location of accidental drownings in the UK   64
Table 7.3: Percentage of population taking part in water-sports (GB, aged
    16+2000)   65
Table 7.4: Selected water sports in UK – a rough indication of relative risk   67
Table 8.1: Reported cases of leptospiral infections in England and Wales, 1990 to
    1995   72
Table 9.1: Most popular outdoor sports (GB, aged 16+2002)   80

List of illustrations

My grandfather trying to teach my grandmother to swim at Ditchford in the
    1930s   xvi
The Boat Picnic   2
Les Baigneuses 1920   9
Bathing in the lake at Victoria Park in the late nineteenth century   16
Competitors in the annual Cambridge Ladies' Swim, August 1960   21
The disused diving platform at Coate Water, summer 2003   74
Swimmers enjoying Henleaze Lake, July 1989   82
Family fun at Keynes Country Park, summer 2003   84
Bathing above the weir at Farleigh Hungerford, summer 1999   110
Boys jumping off Halfpenny Bridge at Lechlade, summer 2003   111

Acknowledgements

Many people have contributed to this book in several different ways.

Marion Shoard's works on access to our countryside have long been a source of inspiration. More immediately, the writings on wild swimming by Roger Deakin and Rob Fryer encouraged me to think that the book might find a receptive audience. I owe them much.

I am grateful, too, to Mark Thompson and other committee members of the Henleaze Swimming Club, Yakov Lev of the Rivers and Lakes Swimming Association, and to the poet, John Freeman, for their advice at an early stage and their warm encouragement.

Since much of the information I needed was not available from published sources, the internet has proved invaluable. I have bombarded many people, usually by email, for information; some ignored my requests, but most responded quickly and helpfully. They include: John Ablitt, Gaynor Aaltonen, Rober Asprey, Susanne Baker, Hugo Blomfield, Paul Bolton, Douglas Caffyn, Will Gibney, Joanna Carter, Crichton Casbon, Mike Clack, Roger Cole, Peter Cornall, John Davies, Suzanne Denness, Ian Drury, Stuart Gibbons, Kate Hedges, Stewart Pomeroy, David Hoar, Paul Hodgson, Zoe Hughes, Gareth Jones, Michelle Little, Carissa Lough, Liz Kendrick, Derek Klemperer, Angela Martelli, Steve Miller, David Moore, Mike Petty, Steven Poolman, Naresh Rao, Tonia Reeve, Crispin Scott, Lesley Sanders; Bob Sharman, Sally Silk, Amanda Strang, Jessica Strudwick, Ali Swainston, Rachel Teal, Simon Tilley, Sharon Waldron, Liz Waters and Steve Webster.

I would also like to thank those who have given permission to use written material or illustrations:

John Freeman for an extract from 'A good day' from *The Light is of Love, I Think*, by John Freeman, Stride 1997.

John Burnside for extracts from 'History' and 'Heatwave' in *The Light Trap*, Jonathan Cape 2002.

John Fuller of the Sycamore Press, for an extract from 'Swimming 1949' by Richard Freeman, Sycamore Press 1980.

Hon Michael J. Beloff and Javan Herberg for permission to refer to the joint advice to the United Swimmers Association *In the Matter of a Proposal for Self-Regulated Swimming in the Hampstead Ponds*.

MORI and the National Trust for permission to refer to findings from *Landscapes in Britain 2004*.

The estate of Gwen Raverat for the drawing *The Boat Picnic* and the woodcut *Les Baigneuses* 1920.

Derek Klemperer for the photograph of Henleaze Lake, July 1989.

Rob Fryer for the photograph of bathers at Farleigh Hungerford, summer 1999.

The *Cambridge Evening News* for the photograph of the competitors in the annual Cambridge Ladies' Swim, August 1960.

I am particularly delighted to be able to thank Daniel Start for his permission to use the cover image. This is one of the many splendid photographs in his first wild swimming book, *Wild Swimming*, published in 2008. For details of this, and his two more recent books, *Wild Swimming Coast* and *Wild Swimming France*, see www.wildswimming.com.

I knew none of these helpers before I started and one of the rewards of this project has been to put me in touch with so many kindred spirits. My greatest debt, however, is to someone I have known for many years: to Hilary Perraton for his encouragement, critical comments and practical help. I owe him more than I can say.

Foreword

W e human beings may have made our home on land, but it was from water that our parent life forms emerged. Perhaps that has something to do with the enthusiasm with which we plunge into, splash around in and swim through water given half a chance. Even in the face of an unforgiving climate, our children run to the water's edge with eyes shining more brightly than at any other time. And why not? Revelling in the embrace of the element which covers most of our planet is one of life's true joys. Surely it ought to be on hand everywhere so all can delight in it whenever they choose.

We take access to water for granted at the seaside. When we get to the tideline, we assume we can swim in the ocean as of right. In fact, the foreshore has owners, but they dare not try and use their property rights to inhibit our access to the waves. For most people, however, the nearest waterside is not the seashore but the edge of one of our vast range of inland waters – lakes and pools, rivers and streams, reservoirs and canals. Owners of the beds and banks of all of these are entitled to exclude the rest of us from their waters, and they feel few inhibitions about using this power to the full.

Landowners and anglers, to whom the former often sub-let rights, claim exclusive use of about 97 per cent of the rivers of England and Wales, according to a study by the University of Brighton in 2001 (University of Brighton 2001: 30). This means that, even in the closed season for angling, owners feel legally justified in barring any other water users, whether swimmers, canoeists, people with rowing boats or children who wish to paddle from entering "their" water. Rivers governed by specific legal public rights of navigation, such as the Thames and the Wye, are exceptions. The effect of this situation is that would-be water users are forced to congregate in small areas, while limitless potential opportunities for the enjoyment of waters elsewhere are denied us. We are missing much.

Dive into an upland pool, and the chill would take your breath away, even in June. On the other hand, the thousands of lakes dotted over the countryside of lowland Britain in counties such as Hampshire and Northamptonshire, Dorset and Lincolnshire, whether gracing extensive private parklands, filling former mineral workings, or lying half-hidden amidst woods and fields, would be more congenial than the sea in early summer because they warm up more quickly. But few of us have any idea what either experience would feel like. In many places, we are not allowed to find out.

The towpaths of most of our canals are freely available to walkers because British Waterways has chosen to promote them as a recreation resource. But our canals, lovely as they are, present nothing approaching the variety of our rivers. We know almost nothing of the swift currents and choppy waters which can give way a hundred yards on to still waters in streams and rivers from Kent to Lancashire and Carmarthenshire to County Down. A river in winter can be utterly unlike the same river in summer. Topographical and geological variation is vast. You may come upon a waterfall, swim under a stretch of cliff, or round a bend to find yourself facing a wide, shallow stretch beside which a dipper is bobbing or the tail of a grey wagtail dancing up and down.

Wade through our rivers and streams and myriad types of waterweed can wrap around your body just as caressingly – or threateningly – as the water itself. Wildlife is closer at hand than in the sea: you can surface from an underwater dive to find yourself eyeball-to-eyeball with a frog sitting on a lily pad. And all this against an ever changing backdrop of bank-side vegetation – perhaps a cluster of stately purple loosestrife and yellow flags, then a steep, muddy bank bearing the paw imprints of an otter and, hot on its heels, creamy drifts of heavily-scented meadowsweet, over-hung by a curtain of weeping willow or presided over by stately aspens, alders and crack willows.

Our exclusion from such delights not only limits opportunities for a wide range of sights, sounds, smells, tactile stimuli and healthy exercise: it also distorts our perception of our country. You could actually put the rivers of Cornwall many, many times around that county's coastline, they are so numerous and long. But how many of us could name them let alone recall their individual characters, even their variety of bridges? How does the Inny differ from the De Lank or the Lynher from the Carey? The vast majority of Cornwall's myriad streams and rivers can legally be glimpsed only at the occasional spot at which a road or a public path happens to abut or cross them. Few of us would even dream of swimming in these waters, when their banks seem so private and out of bounds.

But suppose we had a legal right not only to walk alongside but also to plunge into inland waters? In this fascinating book, Jean Perraton explores the reasons why we should, as well as how some of the real conflicts which might arise with other interests, such as nature conservation, angling and public safety, could be resolved.

The book appears at a particularly interesting moment in the struggle about rights over the environment in Britain and over water in particular. In 2005, one of the first pieces of legislation enacted by the Scottish Parliament, the Land Reform Act 2003, came into effect. This law asserts a public right to be present in and to move freely not just over land but also over bodies of inland water, whether flowing or still, at any time of the day or night. It marks a milestone in the long and often turbulent history of struggle over environment rights in the United Kingdom.

To exercise their new right, Scots must behave responsibly – that is, they must respect the privacy of others, help land managers to work safely and effectively, care for the environment, take responsibility for their actions, keep their dogs under control and take extra care if they are organising an event or running a business. But if they do these things, they can walk along bridges and banks, enter the water whether to wade or swim, and take non-powered craft like rowing boats and canoes in all lochs and rivers, canals and reservoirs, streams, estuaries as well as along the coast; the right applies under water as well as on the surface. A Scottish Outdoor Access Code, published by Scottish Natural Heritage, the main conservation and outdoor recreation government agency north of the border, has set out the framework within which local authorities should assert the public's access rights and sort out any conflicts which may arise (Scottish Natural Heritage 2004).

But the right to roam legislation enacted in 2000 for England and Wales (Countryside Rights of Way Act 2000) is very different. Water was not singled out for mention as it was in Scotland; instead the new right south of the border is restricted only to certain areas of land whose boundaries are marked on maps. An area cannot appear on these maps unless it falls within one of five categories of land; it must consist wholly or predominantly of moorland, heathland, downland or mountain or be registered common land; all told, these types of land cover a maximum of 10 per cent of the surface of England and Wales. Occasionally a piece of water may be included on the maps if it is part and parcel of one of these categories. But if the water involved is not tidal, the rights of the public specifically exclude a right to bathe or use a boat or sailboard (Schedule 2 (1) (b) and (i) CROW Act 2000). The legislation allowed for the possibility that another category of terrain would be covered – coastal land – and in 2012, maps were being drawn up for stretches of coast in pilot areas; a right of access under the 2000 Act over coastal land plainly would not exclude bathing. Northern Ireland has not seen any of these limited extensions of access rights.

Yet Scotland's example is stirring demands elsewhere in Britain for a new approach. So this book comes at a time when we should all be thinking about what access to our environment ought to entail. There is still a long way to go before we can look forward to being able to dip our toes into all our lakes, rivers and streams in the long, hot summers which apparently lie ahead. Reading this book should be an essential step towards that goal.

Marion Shoard, April 2012

Preface to the new edition

Swimming for me has always meant the sea, a river or, when I could find one, a lake. Now we call it wild swimming, and now wild swimming has become cool. When I started to work on the first edition of this book I was reluctant to confess what it was about – if I did, it usually provoked an indulgent smile and change of subject. Since then two lovely books, Daniel Start's *Wild Swimming* and Kate Rew's *Wild Swim*, which came out within a month of each other in 2008, have done much to bring about this remarkable change in public perception. Now each summer we see colourful middle-page spreads in national newspapers, as well as television programmes, celebrating the joys of swimming in lakes and rivers.

In *Wild Swimming*, which builds upon Rob Fryer's pioneering *Directory of Cool Places*, Daniel guides us to some of the finest inland swimming holes in Britain, with interesting commentaries on the adjacent landscape, wildlife and history, and clear instructions on how to find each listed site, as well as warnings about unexpected dangers. His superb photographs entice us to get out and find one. Some are easily accessible, but many of the spots featured in the book are in the remoter areas of the country. For those of us living in towns and cities it is not so easy to find a good place to swim: a place where we are allowed to swim, within easy walking or cycling distance of our homes, somewhere for a quick dip after work, or a more leisurely swim and picnic at the weekend.

That is the problem explored in this book, and it remains much the same on the ground and in the water as it did in 2005. Since then, however, we have seen not only a change in the public perception of wild swimming, but also a significant shift in the attitudes and policies of some of the organisations that, until recently, discouraged us from swimming in lakes and rivers, or discouraged landowners and site operators from allowing us to do so. In this revised edition I have updated many details within the original chapters, and provided pointers to the significant changes in policy and practice. The new Postscript gives more detail on the important changes in policy and practice, and also highlights what has not changed and what still remains to be done.

Introduction

I was born by the sea. My earliest memory is, as a two-year-old, crawling under the new tank traps with my dad, and clinging to his back as he swam out to sea. That was his last swim before the war took him away from us for five long years.

How we missed the sea in our exile to the Midlands during the war. Among the few pleasures that shine out from those grey sad years were summer expeditions across the fields to Ditchford. There, on the little stony beach below a handsome stone bridge, my sister and I would paddle and splash while my mother swam in the brown, polluted waters of the river Nene – the same spot where my father and grandfather learnt to swim. It wasn't the sea – but it was the next best thing. On returning to Eastbourne, we children revelled in long unsupervised summer days on the beach and soon discovered for ourselves how to stay afloat and swim doggy-paddle. It would never have occurred to us, at that time, to seek out a pond or a river in which to swim.

It was more than a decade later that I began to discover the many different flavours of inland swimming. First to be sampled were the relatively warm, placid waters of the river Cam, swimming lazily behind a punt and, once, by moonlight with a boyfriend in Byron's Pool. Later, I discovered the icy pools in the mountain streams of the Lake District and the delight of slithering over smooth black rocks to the pool below, before drying in the sun on soft damp mossy banks. I found, too, the shallow mountain tarns, which get surprisingly warm as their dark peaty bottoms absorb the heat of the sun, where, if they were too small to swim in, I could float on my back and feel part of the world of water boatmen and dancing cotton grass. On returning to Cambridge with a baby son, after a few years in London, it was good to find that we could swim in a pond near the mill at Hinxton. Later still, on warm summer evenings after the children came home from school, we would swim in the Cam at one of the old bathing places on Coe Fen and eat a picnic supper on the river bank. Occasionally we would travel further afield to a picnic spot in the Fens with a lake, the remains of old sand and gravel workings, where we could run down steep sandy banks and jump into the water.

We can still enjoy the mountain streams and tarns, but the springboard and hand rails to the steps into the water have gone from the bathing place on the river Cam. Byron's Pool, with its ugly concrete weir and the drone of motorway traffic, is no longer a peaceful romantic spot. 'No swimming' notices greet us as we approach the pond at Hinxton, its banks overgrown with nettles, and we are no longer allowed to swim in the sandy fenland pool.

In recent decades many changes, not least in the attitude of public authorities, have discouraged swimming in the lakes and rivers of England and Wales. Before the eighteenth century, those who bathed did so mainly in inland waters. Then came the fashion for sea bathing which has remained an important part of our leisure culture. But now, in contrast to most other European countries, many of our lakes and rivers are no longer regarded as places to swim. This book examines why this is so and why it is important that people who wish to swim in inland waters should be able to do so.

Many writers have been enthusiastic swimmers and the book begins by drawing upon their work to convey, far better than I could, the intensity of pleasure and the range of emotions that swimming in lakes and rivers can evoke. Chapter 2 then takes a brief look at the history of swimming in this country acknowledging that we know little about swimming before the eighteenth century, and what we do know is largely limited to the activities of the aristocracy and upper social classes. Also, as background, chapter 3 examines changes in our environment, particularly recent changes to our rivers and riversides, as well as the continuing constraints upon access to inland waters and the lack of rights to bathe in most of them, that make it difficult for people in lowland England to find good places to swim.

The next two chapters look at public policy. Chapter 4 examines the main agencies that control our water environment – the Environment Agency, British Waterways and the Canal and River Trust, and water companies – while chapter 5 looks at the agencies that control or influence the management of land and water for recreation – the countryside agencies, sports councils, Forestry Commission and local authorities. With a few exceptions, in recent years they have all ignored, discouraged or banned swimming in lakes and rivers.

Why is this so? A large part of the explanation lies, as we see in chapter 6, in the legislation relating to the duty of care which owners and managers of sites owe to members of the public who come onto their land, and in the way that this has been interpreted, sometimes over-zealously, by organisations concerned with safety. Chapters 7 and 8 look at what the dangers really are, examining the statistics on drowning and the risks of catching a disease from swimming in untreated waters.

The next three chapters discuss why public authorities should adopt a less restrictive attitude to swimming in lakes and rivers. Chapter 9 seeks to find out whether there really are people who want to immerse themselves in cool, often cold, untreated water now that there are so many heated swimming pools. This is a neglected topic for surveys, but there are indications of an unfulfilled demand. Given the immense pleasure that such swimming can bring, this alone would seem to be a good reason for swimming to be treated more sympathetically by public policy-makers. But, there are other cogent arguments for widening the opportunities for people to swim in lakes and rivers, including the health benefits of outdoor exercise and the low impact that swimming has upon the environment. These are discussed in chapters 10 and 11.

My grandfather trying to teach my grandmother to swim at Ditchford in the 1930s.

The final chapter describes some of the many practical measures that could be taken now to enable more people to enjoy this pleasurable and environmentally benign activity. To make more progress, however, we need a change in attitude to swimming and measures that will relieve owners and managers of land of some of their concerns about litigation. Most importantly, we need a more comprehensive 'right to roam', one that will give us more widespread access to the countryside and a right to swim in its lakes and rivers.

This book is a plea for freedom: freedom to enjoy simple pleasures that do not harm the environment or endanger other people, and freedom to accept the risks of doing so.

1

THE SUMMER'S SOVEREIGN GOOD

I thought the bathing place one of the most beautiful sights in the world: the thin naked boys dancing about in the sunlight on the bright green grass; the splashing, sparkling river; the reckless high dives...

Gwen Raverat *Period Piece* (1960: 108-10)

Bathing: it is the summer's sovereign good.

Gerard Manley Hopkins *Epithalamion* (Gardner 1953: 85)

Not all writers have shared Gerard Manley Hopkins' passion, but many are, or have been, enthusiastic outdoor swimmers. In this chapter I draw upon their work to convey not only the intensity of the pleasure of swimming in lakes and rivers but also the range of emotions that it can engender.

Simply fun

William Wordsworth knew well the delight, and the sense of freedom, of summer swimming.

> Oh! Many a time have I, a five years' Child,
> A naked boy, in one delightful Rill,
> A little Mill-race severed from his stream,
> Made one long bathing of a summer's day,
> Bask'd in the sun, and plunged, and bask'd again.

In this extract from *The Prelude* Wordsworth was recalling his early childhood in Cockermouth, where the garden of his home overlooked the river Derwent – the stream from which the mill-race was severed. Another lover of the Lake District's mountains and lakes, Arthur Ransome, in writing his Swallows and Amazons stories, drew upon memories of boyhood holidays spent on Lake Coniston – fishing, sailing and swimming. His account of the swims that are an everyday part of the children's summer adventures is described in understated and unsentimental, but no less evocative, prose. He tells us, for example, how early one morning John left the other children asleep in their tents and ran down to the landing place, splashed

The Boat Picnic. Drawing by Gwen Raverat from Period Piece (© Estate of Gwen Raverat 2005. All rights reserved, DACS)

out into the water and swam hard for a minute or two, reflecting in his no-nonsense boyish way 'This was better than washing' (Ransome 1962: 100).

Not many youngsters now have the freedom that Wordsworth or Ransome enjoyed in their youth but, happily, there are still opportunities for more-supervised fun at the seaside and sometimes in lakes and rivers. There can be few children who do not revel in the simple pleasure of messing about in water. And it is not just children who paddle and splash in shallow water, laughing and squealing with pure delight. The hilarious scene in E. M. Forster's *A Room with a View* captures the extraordinary effect that water can have on adults when two young men, Freddy and George, and, after some hesitation, the local vicar, Mr Beebe, decide to bathe in a small heathland pond. Mr Beebe, to his relief: 'could detect no parishioners except the pine-trees, rising up steeply on all sides, and gesturing to each other against the blue. How glorious it was! The world of motor-cars and Rural Deans receded illimitably.' (Forster 1909: 199-200) It was not much more than a pond – just ordinary water and not much of it, but ordinary water on a warm day, as nothing else, can free the spirit, turn podgy middle-aged clergymen into young boys again. The bathe turned into a boisterous romp abruptly halted by the unexpected encounter with Freddy's mother, sister and prospective brother-in-law on their more sedate walk through the woods.

In Iris Murdoch's early novel *The Bell* we see the young Toby Gaishe, eager to be in the water, running along the lakeside path and, on reaching the wood, running even faster 'but now for sheer delight, jumping over the long strands of bramble and the hummocks of grass which were growing freely on what used to be the path' (Murdoch 1984: 142). Swimming played a vital part in Iris Murdoch's novels, as in her life, often with symbolic importance. Toby's delight in swimming in the lake reflects his youthful innocence, his freedom from the neuroses and the emotional entanglements which afflict the other characters – as well as his creator's passion.

Libby Purves, I am sure, would have wanted to join Freddy, George and Mr Beebe in their watery romp. She writes of the private, primitive, subversive excitement of giving yourself to the water: 'As you paddle, sloosh, puff, spit, and shake your trailing hair: you are involved in the landscape in a rare and satisfying way. The only dry activity that comes anywhere near it is lying down on a grassy slope and rolling to the bottom' (Purves 2003: 17). Swimming, like rolling down a grassy bank, is fun and, especially for adults, gloriously liberating. There are not many other ways in which, as we grow older, we can join in such basic childish pleasures without feeling comic and unseemly.

In more reflective mood

Swimming in lakes or rivers is often a quieter, more reflective activity, maybe taking place in an out-of-the-way stretch of water in the early morning or late at night. Rose Macaulay, describing an early morning swim somewhere upstream from Cambridge, recalls the sensuous pleasure of gently flowing river water.

> I let the slow flow carry me gently along through shadow and light, between long weedy strands that slimily embrace me as I drift by, between the bobbing white and gold cups and the slippery juicy stems, beneath willows that brush my head with light leaves, beneath banks massed high with may, smelling sharp and sweet above the musky fragrance of the tall cow-parsley. Buttercup fields shine beyond those white banks; the chestnuts lift their candles high against the morning sky (Macaulay 1968: 54).

Early in the morning, or by moonlight after a hot summer's day, the smoothness of the surface of a lowland river can invite a reverential response, one that is not just confined to adults. As a teenager the film director, John Boorman, canoed up the Thames on a hot day to camp on the island of Magna Carta at Runnymede. He recalls awakening 'to a private dawn of fragile stillness' and entering the river 'with reverent care and infinite slowness so as not to disturb its perfect smoothness'. He felt that if he could swim out into it without causing a ripple, he 'would live for ever and great mysteries would be revealed' to him. The experience of that swim was so profound that it inspired him to seek to recapture, though his films, the magic of that day (Boorman 2003: 44-45). He adds that, occasionally, he succeeded.

A similar feeling of reverence overwhelms Tim Reade, in Iris Murdoch's *Nuns and Soldiers*. Coming across a clear still pool, hidden in the cleft of a mountain, he is so moved that, hot as he is, he cannot 'sully that pure water with his sweat or with his gross splashing interrupt its sibylline vibration'. He refrains from swimming, but the experience fills him with happiness and inspires him to paint again. He leaves the pool untouched and decides to swim, instead, in the unattractive and dangerous waters of an irrigation canal (Murdoch 1980: 154-155).

More prosaically, the uncertainty as to what might lie beneath the surface also cautions the experienced river swimmer to enter a river or a lake with care. The boys in Richard Freeman's poem *Swimming 1949* are alerted to the dangers after one of them finds sharp rotted stakes below the reflecting surface:

> And we never again jumped straight into strange water,
> With sweeping hand, like searching the back of a drawer,
> We lowered ourselves carefully in,
> For death can be a small thing,
> And however safe things may appear
> There's nothing safer than a little fear. (Freeman 1980)

Fear makes the boys cautious but does not deter them.

The faster-flowing streams of hillier districts offer a more exhilarating sensation for the bather but these, too, may be approached quietly and cautiously. In Hopkins' unfinished poem *Epithalamion* we see a tense and withdrawn man, avoiding the nearby boisterous bathing boys, slip into the cool water where, released of his clothes, released of his cares, he 'looks about him, laughs, swims'. With those simple words the tension of this poem, tightly packed with elaborate imagery, like the tension of the bather himself, is simply and suddenly gone.

Tension gives way to a deep sense of contentment. Henry Williamson, best known for his novel *Tarka the Otter*, recalls in his memoirs lying still 'in the shallow water, on the golden gravel of the ford, watching the clear cold water foaming over my body, watching it whirling the sand-specks and scooping the stones in little waterfalls and eddies along my length, feeling myself part of the great stream of life, and deeply content for the gift of being alive in the world' (Williamson 1959: 68).

Being part of nature

The feeling of being 'part of the great stream of life', alert to the sights and sounds of the natural world, is widely shared by those who swim in natural waters.

For the conservationist and writer, Roger Deakin, who until his death in 2006 lived more simply and closer to the natural world than most of us, being in the water – river, sea, lake or pond – enabled him to feel 'on equal terms with the animal worlds' around him. His swimming journey across Britain, recounted in *Waterlog*, begins with a swim in the rain in his own moat where, he tells us, 'I can go right up to a frog in the water and it will show more curiosity than fear. The damselflies and dragonflies that crowd the surface of the moat pointedly ignore me, just taking off for a moment to allow me to go by them, then landing again on my wake' (Deakin 2000: 4).

In a letter to his future wife, the nineteenth-century clergyman and author, Charles Kingsley, described how he spent a hot July day:

> Today it is hotter than yesterday, if possible, so I wandered out into the fields, and have been passing the morning in a lonely woodland bath – a little stream that trickles off the moor – with the hum of bees, and the sleepy song of birds around me, and the feeling of the density of life in the myriads of insects and flowers strong upon me, drinking in all the forms of beauty which

lie in the leaves and pebbles, and mossy nooks of damp tree roots, and all the lowly intricacies of nature which no one stoops to see ... And over all, as the cool water trickled on, hovered the delicious sense of childhood, and simplicity, and purity, and peace, which every temporary return to nature gives. (Huxley 1973: 16)

This urge to become part of the natural world is, for some, a spiritual quest. The novelist and biographer, Tim Jeal, quotes a meditation written by his father: 'Be not merely in the river, but become part of it, through its penetration of one's whole being... The purpose of my life is to partake of the same beauty as the stars and trees and flowers' (Jeal 2004: 4).

After dark, in the absence of visual stimuli, the body is ultra-sensitive to the silky feel of water. Moonlight adds magic and mystery. John Burnside, in his poem *Heat Wave*, describes swimming by moonlight after a hot day, when the river water, eel-black and cold

> ... melded in my flesh
> with all the nooks and crannies of the world
> where spawn appears, or changelings slip their skins
> to ripen at the damp edge of the day
> still blurred with mud
> and unrecovered song. (Burnside 2002)

Into another world – perhaps a better world

As we enter the river or lake, whether we jump in with aplomb or slip in more sedately, we move into another world. It is a world where different forces operate to which our bodies must adapt, but which can also bring other, more subtle, changes in mood and attitude. For Deakin it was a simpler place where 'survival, not ambition, or desire, is the dominant aim' (Deakin 2000: 3).

A deep, cold quarry pool lies beneath the hot, rainless summer of Tim Pears' novel *In the Place of Fallen Leaves*. When Alison, the young narrator, swims there – as she often does – she feels herself to be part of the water 'as if this was where I was meant to live ...' (Pears 1993:169). That feeling of belonging to the water, of the water being the real world, is a recurrent theme among those who love swimming. John Boorman comments that he and his daughter, when not in the water, shared 'the same sense of being temporary visitors to earth and air from watery places' (Boorman 2002 : 94).

Water has long been associated in many cultures with redemption and purification, reflecting not only its cleansing properties but also the profound sense of well-being that immersion can bring. It is not surprising that novelists have followed theologians in using swimming as a metaphor for moral development – the washing away of sins or finding moral courage to change one's life, to develop or to break free. A better world, a world of purity and peace, awaits the ill-used little chimney sweep in Charles Kingsley's *The Water Babies*. When Tom climbs down the steep bank of an upland stream to wash his soot-ingrained body, he falls and drowns. The clear cold waters wash away the grubbiness of body and soul and he finds redemption among the water babies.

For Father Golgarty, the central character in George Moore's novel *The Lake*, the swim across the lake marks the end of a spiritual journey and a new beginning. Moore describes the exhilaration of the first lap of the swim to an island where Golgarty 'walked up the shore, his blood in happy circulation, his flesh and brain a-tingle, a little captivated by the vigour of his muscles, and ready and anxious to plunge into the water on the other side, to tire himself if he could, in the mile and a half of gray lake that lay between him and the shore' (Moore 1980: 178). There, a new and more honest life awaits him.

Memories to lighten the darkness

As swimming in rivers and lakes can evoke such intense emotions and such exquisite pleasure, memories of swimming places and particular swimming occasions may remain vivid for many years.

Geoffrey Winthrop Young, who continued to climb and to swim even after losing a leg in the First World War, remembered swimming as a boy from his home on an island in the Thames near Cookham. More than sixty years later he wrote of those days in a letter to his daughter:

> It's odd to wake up these fresh sunshine mornings, to bird song, and feel the stir to run out across the great Formosa meadow, and to the lock of the Odney pool, with the dew wet as rain wetting one's legs from the long buttercups, and the smell of the wet reeds, the Thames' characteristic smell, drying a little in the first sun gleams ... And, lordy-lord! – the incomparable shock of the water as one dived ... the most memorable thrill in living. We must bathe again ... (Hankinson 1995: 18)

Iris Murdoch's biographer, Peter Conradi, recalls that she would plunge into almost any available stretch of water (Conradi 2001: 564). Her husband, John Bayley, maybe not quite as impetuous, also revelled in swimming. So important was this shared pleasure that Bayley begins his memoir of Iris Murdoch, published shortly after her death, by recalling that they would often return to swim in a particular spot in the river even after the Oxford bypass had made it difficult to reach. He describes how they stumbled upon it for the first time nearly forty-five years before. 'We were on bicycles then, and there was little traffic on the unimproved road. Nor did we know where the river was exactly: we just thought it must be somewhere there. And with the ardour of comparative youth we wormed our way through the rank grass and sedge until we almost fell into it, or at least a branch of it. Crouching in the shelter of reeds we tore our clothes off and slipped in like water rats' (Bayley 1998: 4).

Memories such as these bring solace at times of unhappiness. Gerard Manley

Hopkins, in writing *Epithalamion* to celebrate the forthcoming marriage of his brother, needed to evoke a joyous scene. And so he turned to bathing, drawing upon the memories of a bathing place in the river Hodder in Lancashire. This poem was, according to his biographer Norman White, the only poem of unequivocal happiness produced during his five unhappy years in Ireland (White 1992: 425).

The river remained a source of comfort to John Boorman throughout the harsh disciplines of school and the horrors of war, and even as an old man, he tells us in his autobiography, 'when the black dog is on my back, I still summon the consoling river from my childhood and let it flow through my mind, soothing fears and washing away anxiety' (Boorman 2003: 32). He would swim every day in the river that flowed past his home in Ireland, trying to recapture the grace that he knew as a child.

'The past's what you take with you' as Ruby Lennox observes in Kate Atkinson's novel *Behind the Scenes at the Museum* (Atkinson 1995: 331). It is the memory of a swimming day that Frank takes with him to war, and draws upon to help him survive the horror at the bottom of a flooded shell crater. As the battle rages around him, a battle that kills his friend Albert, Frank closes his eyes, pushes himself into the soft mud and concentrates hard on bringing back the day when they first learnt to swim, until

> he could feel the heat of a childhood sun on his skinny nine-year-old shoulders and smell the cow-parsley and hawthorn along the banks of the Ouse. Now he could feel what the water was like when you first stepped into it, the shock of the cold and the strange feeling of his toes splaying out into the mud at the bottom. And he could feel the itchy hemp of the rope that they took it in turns to tie round each other – one splashing out into the river while the other one stood guard, ready to haul him back if he started to sink. And the willow tree in full, silvery-green leaf that trailed in the water like a girl's hair. (Atkinson 1995: 59)

It had been, as Albert had said at the time, 'a right good day'.

Longing to join in

Before the twentieth century, bathing in lakes and rivers was a pleasure denied to many women, at least to those in the upper social classes about whom we know most. Literary references to swimming give the impression that, in Britain at least, swimming was predominantly a male preserve before sea bathing became fashionable in the nineteenth century (Sprawson 1992). The activity seems sufficiently unusual for Lambert of Andres, in the twelfth century, to describe disapprovingly a Flemish lady who is enjoying the fish pond 'not simply to wash or bathe, but to cool herself and move about, along the canals and boundaries of the waters, hither and thither, now swimming prone, now supine; now hidden beneath the waters, now above them' (Orme 1983: 37).

One wonders how many other strong-minded ladies, not to mention ordinary women and girls, enjoyed bathing in fish ponds or rivers away from the eyes of male writers. Thomas Randolph's poem *On Six Maids Bathing Themselves in a River*, written in the early seventeenth century, indicates that some young women were tempted to do so:

> When bashful Day-light once was gone.
> And Night, that hides a blush, came on.
> Six pretty Nymphs to wash away
> The sweating of a summer-day,
> In Cham's fair streams did gently swim
> And naked bathe each curious limbe. (Randolph 1643: 126-7)

The poet comes across the maidens swimming in his local river, the Cam, and as they then accompany him to a tavern nearby, we may surmise that the incident is no classical fantasy but rooted in local reality.

For young Gwen Raverat, writing of her protected Cambridge childhood in the 1890s, such pleasures were certainly not possible:

> All summer, Sheep's Green and Coe Fen were pink with boys, as naked as God made them; for bathing drawers did not exist then; or, at least, not on Sheep's Green ... Now to go Up the River, the goal of all the best picnics, the boats had to go right by the bathing places, which lay on both sides of the narrow stream. These dangerous straits were taken in silence, and at full speed. The Gentlemen were set to the oars – in this context one obviously thinks of them as Gentlemen – and each Lady unfurled a parasol, and, like an ostrich, buried her head in it, and gazed earnestly into its silky depths, until the crisis was past, and the river was decent again. (Raverat 1960: 108)

Gwen Raverat's description conveys an acute sense of longing to join in. However, the shackles of respectability that had kept her Edwardian aunts resolutely behind their sunshades were soon to be eased and, as a young woman, she was able to share the joys of river swimming. She comments then, 'I can't bear to think of all these young beautiful people getting old and tired and stiff in the joints. I don't believe there is anything compensating in age and experience – we are at our very best and most livingest now – from now on the edge will go off our longings and the fierceness of our feelings and we shall no more swim in the Cam ... and we shan't mind much' (Read 2000: 125). The sense of longing – a sensuous languid yearning to slip into the water – lingers still in the woodcut, *Les Baigneuses*, which she created later as a middle-aged woman.

The green meadow and the greenwood side

Whether it is Gwen Raverat's boys frolicking in the sparkling river, Rose Macaulay's swim beneath river banks massed with may blossom or Charles

Kingsley in his cooling woodland bath, the delight springs not just from the activity of bathing but also from the landscape in which it takes place. Outdoor bathing and the landscape are inextricably entwined: the water absorbing and reflecting the light from rocks below or trees and clouds above, the immediate setting of the pool or river, and the views to surrounding fields, woods or hills. As Geoffrey Winthrop Young, in recalling his swims in the Thames, commented, 'Much of the enchantment of a river comes from its duplicating the beauty near or above it in its reflections, and presenting lines and colours which delight us from coming to abrupt endings' (Hankinson 1995: 18).

In *Epithalamion* the setting of the bathing place is an essential part of the bather's delight:

> ... leaf-whelmed somewhere with the hood
> Of some branchy bunchy bushybowered wood,
> Southern Dean or Lancashire clough or Devon cleave,
> That leans along the loins of hills, where a candycoloured, where a
>   gluegold brown
> Marbled river, boisterously beautiful, between
> Roots and rocks is danced and dandled, all in froth and waterblowballs,
>   down.

And, the bather, coming across the rowdy village lads enjoying one delightful pool, finds himself an even lovelier one nearby: a 'Fairyland; silk-beech, scrolled ash, packed sycamore, wild wychelm, hornbeam fretty overstood / By'. Here he hurriedly removes his clothes to swim. It is the setting, leading up to the swim, that Hopkins describes in such intricate detail; after the bather enters the water, the poet falters and the poem was never completed.

In this poem Hopkins was drawing upon memories of happier days bathing in the river near Stoneyhurst in Lancashire – a spot known locally as 'Paradise'. Writing to his mother in June 1871 he told her, 'We bathe every day if we like now at a beautiful spot in the Hodder all between waterfalls and beneath a green meadow and by the greenwood side O. If you stop swimming to look round you see fairyland pictures up and down the stream' (Abbott 1956: 117).

For Rose Macaulay's early-morning swim in the Cam, the setting is perhaps less dramatic but no less magical, and an essential part of the pleasure of her swim. 'The river, pale and secret, slides past, between the green shadow of willows and the grey light of dawn and the white shining of the hanging may-bushes and the deep green of the waving weeds' (Macaulay 1968: 54). D. H. Lawrence, in *Women in Love*, describes two sisters canoeing across a lake to a place where 'a tiny stream flowed into the lake, with reeds and flowery march of pink willow herb' and, with nobody to see them, they 'swam silently and blissfully for a few minutes, circling round their little stream-mouth' (Lawrence 1960: 184).

It is no surprise that the nostalgic utopian landscape of William Morris' *News from Nowhere* includes a scene where barefoot girls are playing in the grass after bathing in the Thames. The narrator of the tale comes across the girls, taking a rest from haymaking, 'on the green lip of the river where the water turns to Goring and Streatley' (Morris 1970: 147). As the landscape is important to the bather so, here, bathing becomes part of the landscape.

The walk to the bathing place

Just as the surroundings of a bathing place can be a vital part of the pleasure of swimming, so too is the route to get there – whether the swim is the goal or an incidental, even unexpected, delight in the course of the walk. Wild swimmers are often enthusiastic and energetic walkers. Both William Wordsworth and Geoffrey Winthrop Young loved long mountain walks. Tim Jeal recalls that his father would 'walk happily for hours, carrying me whenever I flagged, as satisfied to be squelching along muddy paths as climbing the springy turf of sunlit hillsides' (Jeal 2004: 4). The pleasure of walking, like that of bathing, depends upon the landscape and the weather – the sights, the sounds, the smells, and the feel of sun and wind. A good walk and a good bathe go well together.

To come across a clear and unexpected pool in which to swim, or even a shallow shingly stream to wallow in, can turn an ordinary walk into a special day. John Freeman, whose poetry talks simply and directly of landscapes and waterscapes, describes such a day, a magical walk somewhere near Llanwrtyd Wells, when both the route of the walk and the bathing place were unplanned: 'a good day to follow a path up a hill through woods and fields, not knowing where it leads, to walk and sit and walk again and find a fast-flowing river shallow and many-voiced over many-coloured sparkling stones and lie down gasping letting the water roll you gently over' (Freeman: 1997: 106).

The delight of swimming in lakes and rivers – in the open air, among woods or meadows, mountains or moors – lies in moments such as these. They set the scene for this book. The following chapters explore how such moments have become more difficult to experience, why this is so, and what could and should be done to enable more people to enjoy the summer's sovereign good.

2

A QUICK DIP INTO THE
HISTORY OF SWIMMING

... if any scholar should go into any river, pool or other water in the county of Cambridge, by day or night, to swim or wash, he should ... be sharply and severely whipped publicly ...

Pronouncement by the Vice Chancellor of the University of Cambridge
1571 (Cooper 1843: 277)

Eight hardy spirits took the plunge at the Town Bathing Sheds though it took nearly half an hour to break the ice. Many of them have hardly missed a day.

Cambridge News 16 February 1929

The threat of dire punishment was needed to deter the scholars of Cambridge University from swimming in the river Cam in 1571. Three centuries later the river had become a crowded bathing place for town and gown alike. Now, on a warm summer's day, there will be young boys jumping off the footbridge at Coe Fen and, further from the public eye, a sprinkling of bathers at the swimming club a little way upstream, but it is the punts that throng the river. Drive north across the fens to the sea at Hunstanton, however, and you would expect to see people of all ages paddling and splashing and swimming in the brown peaty waters. Yet in Britain sea bathing is a relatively recent phenomenon. Before the seventeenth century, the scanty records suggest that those who washed, bathed or swam, did so in inland waters. Here we take a brief look at the changing patterns of swimming in Britain before exploring, in the next three chapters, some of the reasons why lakes and rivers are now generally not regarded as places to swim.

Swimming in the Middle Ages

What little information there is about swimming in Britain before the sixteenth century begins, when records began, with the Romans. There is plenty of documentary evidence to show that the ancient Romans, like the ancient Greeks, enjoyed swimming in seas, rivers and purpose-built pools, and some evidence to show that when the Romans arrived in this country they continued to swim for military purposes and later, as occupiers, for pleasure (Orme 1983). But the Graeco-Roman delight in water and bathing appears to have been stifled, after the collapse of the Roman Empire, by the spread of Christianity with its very different attitudes to the human body and to water. Even washing came under suspicion as dangerous to health, enfeebling the body and spreading disease. The cold seas round our shores – like the forests and mountains – were seen as threatening, untamed nature. Here, in the great abyss, the humble fishermen would brave the elements for a livelihood and, perhaps, the solitary devout sinner might mortify his flesh, but, according to some accounts, not bathe for pleasure.[1]

However, Nicholas Orme, in his history of early British swimming, cites evidence to suggest that swimming did not altogether cease after the fall of Rome.[2] Evidence from epic poetry indicates that it remained a skill that was practised by the Anglo-Saxon and Viking settlers and perhaps the unconquered Welsh. Being able to swim was regarded as a useful military accomplishment and an indication of male prowess rather than a recreation. It was after the Norman conquest, Orme suggests, that swimming declined in status as a skill among the aristocracy and, with the increasing weight of bodily armour, virtually disappeared as a military skill.

A renaissance in swimming

By the sixteenth century there appears to have been a revival in interest in swimming which may, but we cannot be sure, indicate an increase in the numbers of people who swam in lakes and rivers. Swimming was still seen primarily as a useful survival skill, but it was also recognised as a healthy and enjoyable activity in which even a gentleman could now take part.[3] Swimming techniques, however, were poorly developed and, it seems, drownings were frequent. Concern about the number of undergraduates drowning in the river Cam persuaded Everard Digby, a fellow of St John's College, Cambridge, that an instruction manual was needed. In 1587 Digby published *De Arte Natandi*, the first British treatise on swimming, to raise the art of swimming 'from the depths of ignorance and the dust of oblivion' (Orme 1983: 81). It was written in Latin in order, Orme suggests, to give this neglected activity status and dignity, but this would have limited its readership to the aristocracy, clergy and scholars. A few years later, however, in 1595, Christopher Middleton, probably also a Cambridge scholar, published a much shortened version of Digby's pioneering work in English, for 'the better understanding of those who understand not the Latine *(sic)* tongue' (Orme 1983: 94).

Digby's treatise is in two volumes. The first discusses the theory of swimming and includes some sensible practical advice on when and where to swim. He advises swimmers to choose clear waters where they can see the bottom, to avoid stirring up the muddy sediments and not to swim when the rain is bringing down dung, straw, leaves and 'what filth or unwholesome things else' (Orme 1983: 120). He also warns his readers not to immerse their hot sweaty bodies suddenly in cold water.

The second volume deals with how to swim, with brief instructions (much too brief to be helpful) and line drawings indicating how to enter the water, including how to dive, how to swim on one's front, back, side and under water, how to float and tread water, together with some curious feats such as how to pare one's toe nails while floating in the water. There is, however, no description of our modern breast-stroke or any overarm strokes such as the sidestroke and front crawl, which were developed or introduced much later. The text and the illustrations make it quite clear that Digby is assuming his readers would be swimming in a river.

Orme concludes that, during the period covered by his history, 55BC to AD1719, swimming was practised by a smaller proportion of the population than today and was predominantly a male activity. It has been suggested that it was confined to eccentric aristocrats, but there are hints that perhaps it may have long been enjoyed by people of lower social class.[4] Women generally did not swim – or at least were seldom recorded as doing so. But, again, we have hints from literature, such as the early seventeenth-century poem by Thomas Randolph quoted in chapter 1, suggesting that some females dared to swim, at least surreptitiously, after nightfall or in a secluded spot. And there are even earlier references, in twelfth-century literature, to 'nymphs who gently swim and naked bathe' (Manning-Saunders 1951: 10).

Swimming for most of this period, up to the early eighteenth century, appears to have been confined to lakes, ponds and rivers, with few people, or at least few gentry, swimming in the sea (Orme 1983: 107). But this was about to change.

The rise of sea swimming

In the late seventeenth century people, affluent people, began to bathe in the sea – not for pleasure but for therapeutic purposes. Maybe ordinary men, and perhaps women, living near the coast had long been accustomed to swim in the sea for fun (Corbin 1994: 39). But in 1667 Dr Wittie of Scarborough successfully persuaded his patients of the value of drinking sea water and immersing themselves in the sea. This was simply a continuation of the long tradition in Britain, as on the continent, of visiting inland spas to drink and bathe in the mineral waters, a tradition that had recently experienced a revival; Bath had been rediscovered and Buxton and Harrogate were flourishing (Hern 1967: 3). Other physicians soon seized upon the expanding economic opportunity: among them a Dr Russell who sent his consti-pated patients to drink sea water at Southampton and Brighthelmston, later to become known as Brighton (Lencek and Bosker 1998: 76-8). At first bathing took place in winter, in the early morning, and not all the bathers can have enjoyed the uncomfortable ritual of being pushed under water for the sake of their health, particularly in the bracing resort of Scarborough at a time when our climate was cooler than now.[5] But the new health fad gave those who tried it an opportunity to discover the joys of sea bathing and seaside life. As the watering places of Weymouth, Brighton and Southend-on-Sea enjoyed the patronage of the royal family, holidays by the sea became fashionable and the foundations were laid for the expansion of seaside resorts.

There appears to have been something wonderfully liberating about this new pastime. Whereas bathing in lakes and rivers in England in the eighteenth century, at least among the leisured classes, remained a male preserve, sea bathing was practised by both sexes. Men and women in England bathed naked at the same time and in the same place, and would continue to do so in some resorts until well into the nineteenth century (Lencek and Bosker 1998: 83). In his diary entry for 5 September 1872, the Reverend Francis Kilvert described an early morning bathe at Weston-super-Mare: 'There was a delicious feeling of freedom in stripping in the open air and running down naked to the sea, where the waves were curling white with foam and the red morning sunshine glowing upon naked limbs of the bathers' (Plomer 1969: 262). But not all seaside resorts were as liberated and the freedom to bathe naked would soon be lost in the others. Women had already started wearing voluminous flannel costumes for bathing and, by about 1880, most men would be wearing the 'university costume', a one-piece garment that covered their chests and came down to their thighs (Hern 1967: 24). Except in a few secluded places, the freedom to bathe naked remains lost today – but sea bathing introduced a permanent liberation for women.

The opportunity to enjoy sea bathing was also becoming more widely shared across the social classes. With the expansion of the railways in the mid-nineteenth century, the introduction of bank holidays in 1871, and rising incomes and holidays with pay in the twentieth century, ordinary families could escape from the grim industrial towns to enjoy bathing and the other pleasures of a seaside holiday. By the early twentieth century trains were taking tens of thousands of working-class families to the seaside for their week's holiday: to Skegness and Cleethorpes, Margate and Southend and, above all, to Blackpool (Brailsford 1991: 124). And the popularity of Britain's seaside resorts continued to rise throughout most of the twentieth century – though more slowly in the second half of the century as cheap package holidays enabled many to seek warmer seas and more predictable sunshine.

Baths, bath houses and swimming baths

For most people in inland towns and villages a swim in the sea would remain an occasional day-trip or holiday-week pleasure, and in the big cities it was not easy to find suitable stretches of water in which to bath, bathe or swim. From the eighteenth century on, however, purpose-built pools would increasingly take the place of rivers and ponds for city dwellers, at first for washing and later for swimming.

Baths for washing and bathing and swimming for pleasure have long been closely associated – and, in print, the ambiguity of the term 'bathing' remains. When they settled here the Romans constructed baths, both public and private, in towns, barracks and great houses and, although most of these were small and only suitable for washing and bathing, a few larger pools, big enough for swimming, have been discovered (Orme 1983: 3).

From the sixteenth century we have references to washing and bathing in ponds and rivers. In Cambridge, for example, the ban on swimming and washing in rivers

Bathing in the lake at Victoria Park in the late nineteenth century (Sexby 1898: 555)

and ponds issued by the university authorities in 1571 indicates that it was practised, although we do not know how widely. Some members of the university,
however, were privileged to be able to bath and bathe in private ponds. From at least
as early as the seventeenth century both Emmanuel College and Christ's College
had private pools fed by a conduit from Vicar's Brook, a clear chalk stream rising
from a spring about two and a half miles south of the city (Fox 1937).[6] Scholars
using the pool at Christ's – which was known as 'the bath' – had to make do with
the water that had first been used by Emmanuel men, though one assumes it was
much cleaner than the Cam into which the open sewers flowed.

Less privileged men and boys presumably still made use of the rivers, as perhaps
they had done, unchronicled, for many centuries and would do for years to come.
Leonard Thompson, talking about his childhood as a farm worker in Suffolk around
the beginning of the twentieth century, recalls that 'Boys were washed until they
were about two, then their bodies didn't see water again until they learnt to swim'
(Blythe 1969: 34). A few decades earlier working-class men and boys in London's
East End would wash and swim in the Regent's Canal despite police attempts to stop
them. Concern about the threat of disease posed by the crowded insanitary living
conditions of the East Enders prompted the city fathers, after Victoria Park was
opened in about 1850, to construct a bathing lake for men and boys. The photograph indicates how popular this lake proved to be.

The close association between washing and swimming was continued in the

---

A BATH IN REGENT'S CANAL

Working-class men and boys in Tower Hamlets, in the mid-nineteenth century, used to wash and swim in the dangerous and polluted waters of Regent's Canal. The canal company, after trying unsuccessfully to stop this practice, sought to confine it to summer evenings. Police were brought in to help enforce this rule but, on a hot day, thousands would congregate on the canal bank and outwit the police. A contemporary account describes how the bathers would undress and plunge into the water before the appointed hour of 9 p.m. and, when the constable tried to seize their clothes, friends would run away with them with the constable in pursuit. This left some bathers running around in search of their clothes while others were free to jump into the canal (Poulsen 1976: 47).

When in 1850 Victoria Park was completed – a project designed to improve the health of the poor and to lessen the danger of epidemics spreading to more affluent areas – there was a demand for a bathing lake. The new park had an ornamental lake but, as this was visible to other park users, it was deemed unsuitable for bathing. So a larger lake was constructed, in a secluded spot, where men and boys were allowed to bathe on summer mornings between 4 and 8. Tens of thousands came, so many that the bathers soon complained that the lake was dirtier than the canal (Poulsen 1976:48). A second lake was excavated and later extended. Here 25,000 bathers were counted one summer morning (Sexby 1898: 555). The photograph suggests that this may have been no exaggeration. Later, a diving board and a floating raft were added and a swimming club formed for all-season bathing.

At the beginning of the twentieth century women too wanted a place to bathe. They were allocated the old disused lake, discreetly surrounded by trees and shrubs. Swimming in both lakes soon became organised under the direction of the Amateur Swimming Association and, in 1905, park regulations decreed that all bathers over 10 years old should wear a costume of an ASA-approved design.

Bathing continued in both lakes until 1934 when the London County Council replaced them with a modern open-air swimming pool for mixed bathing. The new pool, opened by Herbert Morrison in 1936, has gone and the large lake now looks dirtier than the canal.

---

indoor swimming baths, where wash tubs and swimming pools were provided under the same roof. In Liverpool, the first public baths built at the end of the eighteenth and in the early nineteenth century, fed by water from the river Mersey, appear to have been used only for washing people and clothes. In 1851, however, the corporation opened the Cornwallis Street Baths, which included both washing and swimming baths. The swimming pool proved so popular that the wash-house space was converted into an additional swimming area. Though the provision of baths was prompted by concerns about hygiene, the bathing water must soon have become even less hygienic than the river water, as the water was pumped in from the Mersey with no filtration or chlorination and the baths were not drained and refilled until the water became too dirty a few days later. The charges for bathing were therefore highest on the first day, when the water was cleaner, and reduced on following days as it became dirtier. The first continuous filtration plant in the Liverpool baths was not introduced until 1909 and chlorination was not installed until 1930 (Ellison and Howe 1997).

It is only recently that we have substituted the term 'swimming baths' for 'swimming pools'. Now, with the growth of the leisure industry, we have 'leisure pools' with flumes and palm trees and water temperatures higher than those in the Caribbean sea: a far cry from the spartan Victorian swimming baths.

Sun-kissed lidos

During the eighteenth and much of the nineteenth centuries people had shunned the midday sun, seeking to bathe in the early morning or late afternoon. Sunshine was regarded as injurious to health and, so long as dark skin was associated with manual labour, pale skin was valued as a sign of class status. This attitude was to change in the late nineteenth and early twentieth century with the 'plein-air movement', celebrating the values of outdoor physical activity, fresh air and sunshine. With it came a rise in the popularity of all forms of open-air swimming and the construction of open-air pools or lidos: pools no longer associated with bath houses, pools purely for fun.

Some early open-air pools, such as the Jesus Green Pool in Cambridge, were excavated alongside a river and filled with river water. Some, like Rickmansworth Aquadrome, were simply reclaimed gravel pits with a few minimal facilities like diving platforms. Others were partial adaptations of pre-existing lakes: hybrids between natural waters and man-made pools. Ruislip Lido, for example, was built in the 1930s within part of a large lake, originally constructed as a feeder for the Grand Junction Canal, by laying a concrete base under the water flanked by two curved piers on either side.[7]

Other pools built in the inter-war years were connected to the public water supply and, sometimes, had their filtered water aerated through an elegant fountain. Many such pools were stylish modern-movement constructions, with pavilions for refreshments and terraces for sunbathing and picnicking or sitting in deckchairs and chatting to friends. Thirty-five open-air pools were constructed in the 1930s in London alone (Worpole 2000). Lidos brought the seaside into the city but, curiously, they were also built and proved popular in several seaside towns, sometimes next to the sea and filled with sea water. The popularity of seaside lidos may partly be explained by the fact that bathing in some resorts was not as free and casual as it is today. Some councils insisted that bathers used bathing huts or changing rooms, for which a charge was made, and some would prohibit bathing during rough seas (Braggs and Harris 2000: 78).

In post-war Britain, however, the open-air pools began to be replaced by indoor heated pools, better suited to year-round swimming in our cool climate. Unheated pools became increasingly dilapidated and many closed. Pressure on the remaining pools continues, but swimmers and conservationists are fighting back. In 2004 the seaside pool at Bude in north Cornwall was threatened as the Health and Safety Executive argued that its cloudy water and uneven bottom rendered it unsafe. But local supporters stepped in and saved it. A few lidos have been restored including the magnificent Tinside Lido, perched on the tip of Plymouth Hoe, which was refurbished following a determined campaign by local enthusiasts (Dyckhoff 2003). The London Pools Campaign is campaigning vigorously on behalf of London's pools, and the Twentieth Century Society is pressing for the best of the survivors to be protected as listed buildings. We still have about a hundred open-air, mostly unheated, pools in Britain which, for some people, offer an altogether more rewarding experience than swimming in a noisy indoor pool.

A golden age of swimming

While swimming in the sea and in purpose-built pools continued to flourish during the nineteenth and into the twentieth century, the tradition of swimming in rivers, lakes and ponds did not wane but also increased in popularity and continued to be popular until well after the Second World War.

In the nineteenth century men and boys were taking part in swimming races in rivers, canals, lakes, swimming baths and the sea, but under no standards rules (Lencek and Bosker 1998). But with the formation of swimming clubs, swimming began to be more organised. In 1869 the Association of London Swimming Clubs was formed to encourage the art of swimming. One of its first moves, in 1869, was to introduce a national championship race over one mile. The association rapidly widened its membership to clubs outside London and evolved (becoming the Metropolitan Swimming Association and then the Swimming Association of Great Britain) into the Amateur Swimming Association (ASA) in 1879.[8] The ASA and its predecessors were active in setting rules and standards and promoting competitive swimming and water polo. The ASA remains the governing body for organised swimming in England today and sets the rules for swimming races, diving competitions and water polo matches, including those that take place in open waters.

Competitive club-based swimming gave impetus to the development of swimming techniques. Swimmers experimented with new strokes, adding to the traditional breaststroke, the underarm sidestroke, the overarm sidestroke, the trudgeon (a sort of overarm breaststroke) and finally, around the beginning of the twentieth century, the much faster crawl. The stamina of swimmers improved too. Captain Webb had become the first man to swim the channel in 1875 and Gertrude Ederle became the first woman to do so in 1926, beating the previous male record by two hours.

Despite swimming baths and lidos, and trips to the seaside, many casual bathers continued to enjoy their local rivers and local councils gave them practical encouragement. In Cambridge, as in other towns, the corporation provided steps

A RIVER FOR TOWN AND GOWN

Few short stretches of river can have been so well documented and so cele-brated in literature as the three miles between Cambridge and Grantchester.

We know that the from time to time the university authorities tried to discourage undergraduates from bathing in the river that inspired Digby's pioneering treatise on swimming. But we know little of the many ordinary people who must have enjoyed its waters before the nineteenth century. By then official attitudes to river-bathing had changed and the council provided separate bathing huts for men and women of the town. The bathing places were just upstream of the city at Coe Fen and Sheep's Green for, until the Cheddars Lane pumping station was opened in 1895, the river below stank of sewage. After that, a race through the 'The Backs' became a popular annual event until it ceased in the 1980s amid fears of pollution.

On Sheep's Green, in the early years of the last century, the custodian of the bathing sheds, the ebullient Charlie Driver, gave instruction in the finer arts of swimming. He ensured children could swim across the leat before being allowed in the main river. Charlie saved many lives for which, in 1903, he was presented with a purse of gold by members of the Cambridge Amateur Swimming Club.[9]

Meanwhile famous literary figures would swim further upstream, beyond Tennyson's 'long fields of barley and of rye'. Byron's Pool and the Mill Pond in Grantchester were favourite places for Lord Byron and, later, Rupert Brooke, Virginia Woolf and Gwen Raverat. Ludwig Wittgenstein would also swim there. Rose Macaulay could slip quietly into the river Granta, just before it joins the Cam, from the family boat house at the bottom of her garden.

The river at the old bathing places is no longer pink with summer bathing boys. The springboard and the hand rails to the steps that led into the water were removed when the council decided the river was too polluted for swimming. The Cambridge Canoe Club now occupies the site of the old bathing sheds. But a little way upstream members of the Newnham Riverbank Club swim from a secluded stretch of riverbank, often to the surprise and amusement of passing punters, and anyone is free to swim further upstream at Grantchester Meadows despite the increasing weediness of the river and the steep banks and stinging nettles that make it difficult to get in and out.

into the river and sheds for changing, first for men and later, in August 1896, for women. Women and girls could now enjoy what had previously been largely a male pleasure. In Victoria Park, at the beginning of the twentieth century, the women were at last allowed to use the old secluded bathing lake after a larger lake had been constructed for the men (see box on page 17).

Swimming in the river was a popular family activity in the 1920s and 1930s. At this time so many bathers travelled to Ditchford to swim in the river Nene on a

Competitors in the annual Cambridge Ladies' Swim, August 1960 (© *Cambridge Evening News*)

summer weekend that it became known as 'Ditchford-on-Sea' (Phillips 1997). That was before the station, and later the railway line, were closed. Swimmers thronged the other lowland rivers including the river Cam in and above Cambridge.[9] While famous literary figures bathed naked in more secluded spots upstream from Cambridge, ordinary men and women in bathing costumes were swimming at Sheep's Green and Coe Fen and some were joining river swimming clubs and taking part in races and galas. And it was not just in summer; throughout the big freeze of February 1929 the Cambridge News gave reports of people skating and cycling on the frozen river and of swimmers breaking the ice for their daily dips.

And now?

Swimming continues to be immensely popular; more people swim than take part in any other active recreational activity apart from outdoor walking. While most swimming now takes place in indoor heated and chlorinated pools, swimming in the sea is still regarded as normal and legitimate. River swimming remained popular until the 1960s or 1970s, but since then has become, in many places, a rather unusual thing to do. In rivers and lakes where people used to swim, it is now forbidden or at least discouraged; in other places it is no longer possible, or attractive, to swim because of changes to the water environment or the land around. In many places that would be ideal for swimming, such as some of the recently created gravel-extraction lakes, we find people can enjoy a range of new water sports, but not the traditional simple activity of swimming.

An instruction manual on swimming published in 1950 claimed that, 'Today there are few people who need be debarred from the pleasures of bathing. If you live on the coast your problem is merely that of choosing the most desirable stretch of water; if you are in some quiet, inland district there will almost certainly be a stream, or lake, or pool, available; while, if you reside in the large town, indoor baths will most likely afford all-year-round facilities' (Hedges 1950:12). Maybe the author painted a somewhat too rosy picture of the opportunities for inland bathing in his day; he certainly appeared to be unconcerned about the pollution that was widespread then. But it is not a picture that we would recognise today. The next chapters explore some of the reasons why this is so.

3

LOST OPPORTUNITIES AND CONTINUING CONSTRAINTS

One of the things which has been lost is the ability to paddle and even swim in rivers and streams. Today, you rarely see anyone swimming in the British rivers in which country children learned to swim.

Marion Shoard *A Right to Roam* 1999: 91

I am glad to have known our countryside before its roads were too dangerous to walk on and its rivers too dirty to bathe in, before its butterflies were decimated with arsenical spray, before Shakespeare's Avon frothed with detergents and the fish floated belly-up in the Cam.

E. M. Forster Preface to 1960 edition of *The Longest Journey*

People do still swim in lakes and rivers. In his *Directory of Cool Places* Rob Fryer describes over 300 inland swimming places in England and Wales which he or his friends enjoy (Fryer 2009).[1] But many of these are isolated spots, sought-out by the enthusiast. The heyday of river swimming clubs and swimming races is over.

This is hardly surprising. We now have so many more ways in which to spend our leisure time than we had even half a century ago. The growth in car ownership and air travel have given us the freedom to seek our recreation further and further afield. Swimming is still an immensely popular activity but we are now able to use, and are encouraged to use, heated, chlorinated and supervised pools. Many people, probably most, prefer them. But for those who, on a warm summer's day, would like to be able to paddle or swim in a nearby lake or river in the open air, surrounded by grass and trees, the opportunities to do so have diminished.

There are probably many reasons why this is so, not least the changing attitudes of public authorities towards freshwater swimming which are explored in the next two chapters. In this chapter, however, we look at some of the changes in our environment that have also made it more difficult, at least in lowland England, to find attractive places to swim, and the continuing constraints that may prevent us from swimming when we do find an idyllic spot.

River works and agricultural changes

The rivers of England and Wales have been considerably modified, at least since Roman times, to aid navigation, provide water power and improve land for cultivation. Some of the early changes to rivers, such as the construction of weirs for fishing and for water mills, left a legacy of deep pools and millponds which proved a blessing for later swimmers. During the nineteenth century the pace of change increased to meet the water needs of our rising population, to protect urban areas from flooding and to drain agricultural land. As our towns and cities expanded some rivers disappeared completely into underground culverts and others became little more than open drains. Industrial development on low-lying riverside land often cut people off from their rivers. The loss of rural land to urban uses, and the accompanying changes to rivers, continued throughout the twentieth century; it is estimated that between 1945 and 1990 705,000 hectares of rural land were lost to urban development, an area about the size of Greater London, Berkshire, Hertfordshire and Oxfordshire combined (Sinclair 1992). And with urbanisation came the need to protect people and property from flooding. Meanwhile, in the countryside the industrialisation of agriculture, during the second half of the twentieth century, was accompanied by widespread drainage works, especially in eastern England. Under the impetus of post-war concern about food production, rivers had to be straightened and flood plains drained to extend the grazing season or to bring land into arable production.

River works – widening, deepening, straightening, embanking, culverting and diverting – have had profound effects on wildlife and the attractiveness of rivers and have also made them less suitable for swimming. One study of an agricultural improvement scheme found that more than three-quarters of the valuable landscape features – trees, bushes, river shoals, river bends and river cliffs – had been removed (Penning-Rowsell *et al.* 1986: 133). Such changes to a river not only affect the landscape and the wildlife, they also do away with the shallow riffles and the associated deeper pools in which it may be good to bathe. Rob Fryer's directory records the loss of several well-loved bathing spots as a result of recent river works, including Mount Mill Pond near Warminster which disappeared when the river was straightened in the 1970s (Fryer 2003: 39). We do not know how many other bathing places may have disappeared in this way.

The changes in agriculture during the second half of the twentieth century also helped to degrade rivers and their landscape setting. Run-off from artificial fertilisers, rich in nitrates, has increased the growth of weeds and algae in some rivers and lakes. The removal of riverside trees, the failure to pollard in the traditional manner and intensive cropping hard up to the river banks has, in areas of large-scale arable cultivation, degraded riverside landscapes. Few would want to swim in a dredged channel with steep sides, where the ploughed field comes up to the river bank or where the water is carpeted with duckweed.

Now some of these changes are being reversed. New regulations require uncultivated strips to be left between cultivated fields and watercourses. A few rivers and

A LAND OF LOST LAKES AND RIVERS

'The wind, which in the autumn of 1851 was curling the blue waters of the lake, in the autumn of 1853 was blowing in the same place over fields of yellow corn.' William Wells, a local landowner was writing about Whittlesey Mere, once the second largest lake in England (Godwin 1978: 9). Although the draining of the vast wetlands of eastern England, the Fens, had been going on at least since Roman times with 'cuts' short-circuiting the winding rivers, several meres persisted until the nineteenth century before finally coming under the plough.

The meres had long been rich sources of fish and wildfowl and, in the eighteenth century, Whittlesey Mere was also a playground for the wealthy. Lord Orford's diary of 1774 records an expedition in sailing boats to the mere for fishing and partying at a time when the local gentry owned summer houses on its banks. The mere provided splendid skating in winter and, in summer, its clear waters must have made it a good place to swim. Charles Kingsley wrote nostalgically of the 'shining meres, the golden reed-beds, the countless water-fowl, the strange gaudy insects, the wild-nature, the mystery, the majesty ... which haunted the deep fens for many a hundred years (Kingsley 1873: 95). But he accepted that drainage would bring blessings, not least the end of the ague that plagued the local people.

The rich peat soils certainly brought economic blessings to the landowning farmers. But with dehydration and intensive cultivation, the peat has been steadily wasting away; these high-quality soils are a diminishing resource. Plans are now afoot to re-create large areas of wet fen. The National Trust envisages that, eventually, a mosaic of open water, reed beds, wet grassland and wet woodland will stretch from its nature reserve at Wicken Fen, a remnant of wet fen, as far as the northern edge of Cambridge. The local Wildlife Trust, in its Great Fen Project, has embarked on a similar programme to link Woodwalton Fen, another protected remnant of undrained fen, to Holme Fen. These new wetlands will give the threatened species of flora and fauna the space they need to survive. They will also be places for people to enjoy: delightful places where, one hopes, there will be nothing to stop the occasional bather from slipping into the clear waters.

streams have been restored to a more natural state. Trees are being planted, willows pollarded, wet meadows and wetlands are being created (see box 'A Land of Lost Lakes and Rivers'). But more needs to be done.

Water abstraction

As our population has grown and standards of living have risen, our demands upon rivers for domestic water supplies have increased. Use of river water for agricultural irrigation adds to these demands which, in parts of lowland England, has reduced the flow of rivers and, in some cases, turned clear, flowing streams into muddy ditches.

Many studies have drawn attention to the serious and widespread effects of abstraction and drainage schemes on wildlife habitats (Langford and Hill 1992, Fowler 1997). Few accounts mention the effects on bathing places. Desmond Hawkins, however, in his study of the changes to two small tributaries of the river Cam near Cambridge, recalls that within living memory both the Great Wilbraham River and the Little Wilbraham River provided power for water mills, supported shoals of fish and abundant wildlife, and were also used for bathing and boating excursions (Hawkins 2000: 52). Now, as a consequence of drainage works and water abstraction for the expanding city nearby, the Great Wilbraham River has gone and the Little Wilbraham River is more like a drainage ditch than a river. Meanwhile, upstream from Cambridge, on a branch of the river Granta, the villagers at Linton abandoned swimming in the river 40 years ago when its level became too low.

Not all recent changes to rivers, of course, have made them less suitable for bathing. During the nineteenth century, especially in upland areas, some were dammed to create surface reservoirs for drinking water, and further reservoirs were created later in the twentieth century in lowland England. Some of these could provide opportunities for swimming were it allowed by the water companies that control them.

Increasing concerns about pollution

When E. M. Forster, writing in 1960, regretted that rivers had become too dirty to bathe in, river pollution was much worse than it is today. After a slow start, the 1974 Control of Pollution Act has brought about a gradual improvement in water quality in all parts of the country. During the nineteenth century, and well into the twentieth, pollution from industrial effluent and human sewage caused increasing levels of pollution which, in many places, reached a peak in the middle of the last century. The tidal Thames, which had a productive fishing industry at the beginning of the nineteenth century, degenerated into a sewage-polluted drain with no established fish populations by the middle of that century. The water has improved since then and the fish have returned (Environment Agency 2001: 23). Similarly, salmon disappeared from the Mersey in the 1890s and have now returned. By the year 2000, 94 per cent of the rivers in England were judged to be 'good' or 'fair' in terms of their chemical quality, and over 90 per cent 'good' or 'fair' in terms of biological quality (Countryside Agency 2002). These improvements reflect stricter controls on the discharge of pollutants and investment in better sewage works, as well as a decline in polluting industries. There is more, of course, to be done. There are still problems of intermittent discharges of untreated sewage at times of flooding, but it is the continuous and widespread run-off from agriculture – from fertilizers, herbicides and pesticides – which remains the major polluter of rivers today. The enrichment of surface waters by nitrogen from agricultural pollution, and phosphates from sewage disposal, also causes periodic blooms of blue-green algae in some lowland lakes. But overall our rivers are gradually becoming cleaner, and many of our lakes have good quality water and, as we shall see in the next chapter, would comply with the standards of the EC Bathing Water Directive.

As the quality of river water improved, however, concerns about pollution have increased. These two trends are related, of course: public concern about pollution has been an important factor in bringing about the improvements in water quality that we have seen. Although many rivers and lakes are clean enough for water sports, there is a widespread perception that they are dangerously polluted (University of Brighton 2001: para 9.9). Surveys of public concerns about the environment have consistently put water pollution high on the list of worries. In the late 1980s the discharge of chemicals into rivers was found to be the most important of these, followed by the discharge of sewage into coastal waters (HMSO 1990). A later survey found people were much more worried about the pollution of rivers and bathing beaches than, for example, about the more widely publicised suspicions of genetically modified foods. Such perceptions deter them from swimming; about a quarter of respondents in the second survey said they avoided swimming in the sea, rivers and lakes for this reason (DEFRA 2002: para. 9.9). These fears have not been allayed, so that many people still think our rivers are too dirty to swim in.

Increasing concerns about pollution are one of the reasons why local authorities and other organisations have sought to discourage swimming through by-laws and bans on swimming in country parks even, sometimes, where the water quality is relatively good. It is ironic that more people used to swim when rivers were much dirtier, and that moves to discourage swimming have increased as the river water quality has been improving. The annual river swim through Cambridge, which had taken place for about 50 years, was abandoned in late 1980s; now that the water is cleaner the city council still considers it too polluted for swimming. Soon after the war people enjoyed swimming in the Thames, downstream from London Bridge; few would do so today although the river is much cleaner.

Access to lakes and rivers

Not all rivers have been damaged by drainage works; not all riversides and lakesides are denuded by industrial farming. Many of our rivers and lakes are set in beautiful countryside; many of our rivers, and particularly our lakes, are clean enough to swim in. But can we get to them?

Access to the countryside in lowland England is limited for most of us to public rights of way. Our invaluable network of public footpaths and bridleways tends to link village to village, crossing rivers rather than running beside them. The main exceptions are those rivers and canals that were used by horse-drawn barges, such as the Thames, where the public now often enjoys a right to walk along the towpaths.[2] But some of the finest river valleys in lowland England, such as those of the Test and the Rother, are largely inaccessible to the walker and therefore to the swimmer. The people of Cambridge can follow the Cam upstream for about three miles to Byron's Pool, but thereafter the main river and its tributaries are largely inaccessible except where crossed by a road or footpath. Lakes in lowland counties tend to be even more inaccessible than rivers. Private parklands, for example, may have a public footpath crossing the land but, typically, there are no rights of public access to the lovely lakes that grace their grounds. New lakes are constantly being created, through sand and gravel workings, but are often leased to private fishing or water-sports clubs with little general public access (Shoard 1999: 95).

Despite the promise of the National Parks and Access to the Countryside (NPAC) Act 1949 relatively little was done during the following half century to extend our legal rights of access to the countryside. Established rights of way were lost in the process of drawing up definitive maps in the 1950s, a task which was largely executed by parish councils on behalf of county councils, both dominated by rural landowners (Shoard 1997: 268-273). The NPAC Act 1949 had envisaged that gaps in the network of public paths would be filled in, for the act empowered local authorities to negotiate access agreements with private landowners and to make access orders, but these powers resulted in only modest extensions of access to land, largely to mountain and moorland within the national parks. While the 1968 Countryside Act made it possible to extend access agreements and orders over water, this provision does not appear to have been used to improve access to inland waters (University of Brighton 2001: para 2.12.1). In fact, countryside policy during the 1970s became dominated by forecasts of an explosion in demand for countryside recreation and fears that the farmed countryside would be overwhelmed by invasions from the towns; it sought, therefore, to control access rather than to help people enjoy the countryside more freely (Curry 1994, Shoard 1997).[3] The explosion in demand never materialised, and gradually the emphasis of policy makers changed towards helping people to explore the countryside, albeit mainly through information about, and waymarking of, existing rights of way, rather than through the widespread creation of new rights.[4]

The picture is not an entirely gloomy one for, in recent decades, land-owning bodies like the Forestry Commission and the water companies have invited the public to enjoy their land. Environmental charities, such as wildlife trusts and the Woodland Trust, have increased their land holdings with grants from the National Lottery and welcome people on to their sites. Payments to individual farmers through various agro-environmental schemes and to landowners through various tax exemption arrangements have also extended permitted access to rural land, but these arrangements are often of limited value since they reflect the interests of individual farmers and landowners rather than the needs or wishes of the public who, indeed, may be unaware of their existence (Bentley 2001). Extension of access to parklands through inheritance tax agreements may exclude much of the grounds, giving people tantalising glimpses of the woods and the lakes, but not access to them (Shoard 1999: 82-84). The most significant extension of legal rights of access came with the implementation of the Countryside and Rights of Way (CROW) Act 2000, giving us a right of access on foot to open countryside in England and Wales – mountain, moor, heath, down and registered common land – where this was

A LONG, ACCESSIBLE SWIMMING RIVER

'Pox take the boats! Amen' wrote Jonathan Swift to Esther Johnson in 1711 (Swift 1974: 287). He was irritated by the boats that got in the way of a late-night swim in the Thames at Chelsea. This long river, which for centuries has drained fields and towns, supplied them with water, carried away their effluents, provided power for mills, fish for monasteries and a highway for freight traffic, and now increasingly accommodates leisure boats and anglers as well as walkers along its towpaths, has also long been enjoyed by swimmers.

Such uses were often in conflict. In medieval times the construction of weirs for mills and fisheries was a cause of disputes with navigation interests. The river's important role in removing effluent became a major nuisance in the nineteenth and early twentieth century, particularly in the tidal reaches through London. Outside the Houses of Parliament the Great Stink of 1858 drove MPs from sitting in their chambers overlooking the river. It was still pretty foul in the 1930s when the campaigning MP and river-lover, A. P. Herbert, swam from Waterloo to Westminster Bridge. He was well-known as a regular swimmer in those insalubrious waters and boatmen would point him out to their passengers as 'Mr A. P Haddock' – one of the sights of London (Herbert 1936: 109).

Herbert, in his work with the former Thames Conservancy, had championed the idea of a long-distance footpath beside the river. Now a waymarked route runs, mostly on old towpaths, for over 180 miles between its source at Thames Head to the Thames Barrage, enabling people to walk and find some of the many good places to swim. Rob Fryer's directory mentions, among others, Lechlade, in the middle of the village; the Round House, a little further upstream where the Coln joins the Thames; Rushey Weir Pool near Farringdon; Cliften Hampden, east of Abingdon, and Wallingford (Fryer 2009). Some of these spots were also enjoyed by Paul Gedge and the boys and girls from poor backgrounds that he used to take up-river in small rowing boats, camping and swimming on the way (Gedge 1947). His list of essential kit included bathing things but no mention of lifejackets. That was soon after the last World War. Were such a trip to be made today, buoyancy aids would have to be worn at all times – and the plans would be unlikely to include swimming.

defined as 'access land'. Some of these areas had long been enjoyed *de facto* but not *de jure*, and the act does little to improve access to much of lowland England where most people live. It does not enable them to explore more of the gentle lowland landscapes, landscapes that it seems many people actually prefer to the bleaker mountains or moorlands. It does not give them many more opportunities to find accessible green spaces close to their homes which may be more important to them than an occasional trip to more spectacular countryside.[5]

Whereas people are now welcome on some stretches of countryside where previously they had no legal right to be, there is much anecdotal evidence that, more generally, the attitudes of landowners to the informal access previously enjoyed by country people have hardened. Marion Shoard, writing in 1979, recalled that 20 years earlier 'children happily cycled the six miles from Ramsgate to picnic on the grassy meadows then grazed by cows and to catch a jam-jar full of teeming life of the dykes .... Then there was *de facto* access to most of the Minster marshes'. Later, drainage of the marshes, removal of woodlands and ploughing up of the land removed many of the dykes and the farmer prohibited access to those that remained (Shoard 1979: 70). Shoard talked to people who were living in the eastern counties in the 1940s, who could walk freely over meadows once the hay had been cut, picnicking and gathering mushrooms in grazing fields. I too remember, when living in a small East Midlands town, spending late-summer days with my grandmother and neighbours gleaning ears of wheat for the chickens, and later picking blackberries and searching for mushrooms, with no concerns about trespassing. Now, like most people, I keep strictly to public rights of way.

There are, of course, many attractive stretches of river, and some lakes, that are easily accessible by public rights of way. Long-distance footpaths now give access to most of the river Thames, from its official source at Thames Head to the Thames Barrage, and to significant sections of some other rivers, such as the (Welsh) river Wye, enabling people to enjoy walking beside these long rivers and sometimes to find some good swimming places (see box 'A Long, Accessible Swimming River').

Rights to swim

Even when we can reach a lake or river, we may have no right to swim there. At the seaside we have a right to swim in most tidal waters, subject to by-laws that may prohibit swimming. There is no general right to swim in non-tidal rivers and lakes. The legal position for swimmers in inland waters in England and Wales is complicated and uncertain, as it is for other water users. It appears that local people can claim a right to swim in certain places through historic use and, in some cases, the public may swim where there are public navigation rights (Bates 1999). But public navigation rights apply to only three per cent of rivers (University of Brighton 2001: 30). This, however, is disputed. Douglas Caffyn argues that we have a common law right to take a boat along all physically navigable rivers, but his thesis has yet to be determined in the courts (Caffyn 2004).

Here, unlike in many other European countries, the owners of the bank also own half the river bed, giving them certain rights over the use of water, including usually the exclusive right to fish and, provided swimming is not an established use, the right to prohibit people from swimming. The owner of the land surrounding a pond or lake has similar rights. Some lakes may be registered as common land, but this does not necessarily imply a right to swim in them; the 'rights of common' may relate to fishing but not swimming.[6] Where landowners have not indicated their willingness to allow swimming in their waters, swimmers could be trespassing.

Whether, in practice, swimming in lakes or rivers is tolerated by the landowner may depend on whether the waters are leased out for fishing or other income-generating uses. The concern of landowners to protect their fishing interests, and anglers to protect their sport, appears to be an increasing constraint upon swimming in lakes and rivers. But this is not the only problem. Landowners also feel constrained by legislation relating to the duty of care they owe to people who come onto their land, and the way these duties have been interpreted by health and safety watchdogs. This has been the major reason why managers of recreation sites, such as country parks, ban swimming in places even where it used to take place, and why landowners are reluctant to allow swimming in their waters. We look at these issues in the following chapters.

It is possible, of course, to lease the right to use private waters. Swimming clubs could, though rarely do, lease waterside land, enabling their members to swim – but this does not benefit the casual swimmer. Angling clubs have been the most successful groups in securing access for their members, but even so it is estimated that such private arrangements enable those engaged in water-based sports to use no more than 2 per cent of the main rivers and lakes in England and Wales (University of Brighton 2001: 12). Other water users, such as canoeists and sailors, feel aggrieved at the difficulties involved in getting access to inland waters, and the British Canoe Union is currently waging a campaign to secure wider access for canoeists and for other groups such as sailors and swimmers.

Even the new right to roam legislation does not extend our rights to swim, canoe or sail. The interests of landowners and anglers appear to have been powerful in ensuring that the CROW Act 2000, unlike the more radical Land Reform (Scotland) Act 2003 in Scotland, does not extend significantly the right of access to lakes and riversides in England and Wales and does not give people a right to use the waters that come within the defined access areas.[7] The act may enable people to reach the banks of some rivers and lakes that were previously inaccessible, but Schedule 2 of the act specifically excludes people from bathing in, or using a vessel or sailboard on, any non-tidal waters within the access lands.

These continuing, and in some ways worsening, constraints on access to land and water posed few problems for those early twentieth-century writers quoted in the first chapter, many of whom came from privileged social backgrounds with access to lakes and rivers through land ownership and social connections. Rose Macaulay swam in the river Granta from the boathouse at the bottom of the garden of the family home in Great Shelford near Cambridge. It is not something that the ordinary people of the village could easily do now, since there is almost no public access to this stretch of river as it flows past their village. Young public school boys learnt to swim in private stretches of rivers or lakes within the extensive grounds of their boarding schools. Geoffrey Winthrop Young swam from the family home on an island in the Thames and swam in the Thames at Eton, where the college owned five bathing places on the river enabling many boys to develop a love of river swimming (Sprawson 1992: 84). Gwen Raverat's husband, Jacques, was a pupil at Bedales where, after playing cricket in white flannels the boys would race to the pond and bathe 'amid a tumult of joyful shouting' (Spalding 2001: 132). Such lakes, which tend to be less polluted and free from the strong currents that make some rivers dangerous for swimming, continue to be out-of-bounds for most of us today.

The trends and constraints discussed here reflect economic forces and a policy agenda largely unrelated to the question of swimming. The opportunities to swim in lakes and rivers are affected, more directly, by the policies of various public agencies, particularly those that own and manage land. We look at these in the next two chapters, before exploring further the implications of the duty of care.

4

GUARDIANS OF THE WATER ENVIRONMENT

No man shall lett out there sesterns or other noysome synkes untill eight of the clock at night uppon payne for every one doinge the contrary to forfeite unto the Lord for every tyme xiid.

Foxton Bury village by-law of 1594 (Rowland Parker 1772: 150)

Get a life – get a fishing rod!

Environment Agency, *Cambridge Evening News* 2003

Down the centuries parishes, boards of works, fisheries boards and river boards, river authorities and water authorities have tried to keep our streams and rivers clean. The sixteenth century by-law enacted in the village of Foxton Bury, now Foxton in Cambridgeshire, was just one of many such regulations passed by the parish authorities in a constant struggle to stop sewage being emptied into the brook that provided the villagers with water for drinking and for washing. We do not know whether the men and boys of Foxton Bury also found time to bathe in the brook, downstream of the village, before it flowed on to join the Cam in which the more privileged scholars of Cambridge would swim.

Now the agencies that help to keep our inland waters clean also have responsibilities for opening them up for people to enjoy. In this chapter we look at the main agencies that control or influence the use of inland waters for recreation. They include the: Environment Agency which, in addition to its many land-based functions and controls on water pollution, has an important remit for water-based recreation; British Waterways, until 2012, the navigation authority for most canals and some rivers in Britain; the water companies, responsible for water supply and sewage disposal, that also have obligations to enable people to enjoy their reservoirs and the land around them; and the European Commission to whom we owe the Bathing Water Directive in addition to other directives that protect our water environment. This chapter examines how these agencies have influenced the opportunities for swimming and other water-based activities.

The Environment Agency

The Environment Agency, whose remit covers England and Wales, inherited from the National Rivers Authority a general duty to promote the use of inland and coastal waters and associated land for recreation.[1] It would therefore seem reasonable to expect that it might devote some of its energies and resources to improving conditions for swimming in suitable inland as well as coastal waters.

The agency's main effort, in terms of promoting recreation, goes to support fishing. This reflects its more specific duty to maintain, improve and develop salmon fisheries, trout fisheries, freshwater fisheries and eel fisheries, so that 'everyone will have the opportunity to experience a diverse range of good quality fishing' (University of Brighton 2002). It is not surprising, therefore, that an important part of the agency's activities involves protecting fish stocks. But it goes much further and actively promotes the sport of fishing and angling. In addition to stocking waters with fish and improving access to fishing sites, the agency encourages more people, especially young people from disadvantaged groups, to take up angling. A recent corporate plan talks about promoting angling opportunities and supporting novice anglers, developing coaching schemes for 25,000 young people in association with the angling governing bodies, publishing regional guides on where to fish, and creating and developing fisheries close to centres of population (Environment Agency n.d.(b): 21).

The size of the agency's budget devoted to fisheries, compared to spending on conservation and other recreational activities, demonstrates the priority that it gives to fishing. The Corporate Plan for 2004/05, for example, allocated nearly five times as much to fishing as to conservation projects, and more than twice as much as to recreational activities (assuming that the navigation budget mainly benefits pleasure boaters). This pattern of expenditure had been fairly consistent over previous years, although the percentage going to navigation and conservation increased slightly at the expense of fisheries and other recreational spending. In subsequent years the expenditure on navigation continued to increase, while the small share going to other forms of recreation decreased.[2]

Table 4.1: Environment Agency: budget for recreation-related activities 2004/05 (£m)

Sector	Expenditure	Income	Public subsidy
Fisheries	27.1	17.2	9.8
Navigation (pleasure and freight)	11.3	4.2	7.1
Recreation	2.1	0.2	1.9
Conservation	5.9	0.0	5.9

Source: Environment Agency Corporate Plan 2003/06

Fishing brings in significant income for the agency through rod licences and boating generates income through registration fees, mooring fees and other charges, whereas conservation projects usually bring in no income and other recreational activities bring in very little. These charges, however, do not cover the costs. Table 4.1 shows that a greater amount of public subsidy goes to support fishing than conservation, and about the same amount as all other recreational activities together.

The Institute of Leisure and Amenity Management has described the special legal status of fishing as 'inappropriate and ill-advised' and this bias towards fishing has been criticised by organisations representing people engaged in other water sports (University of Brighton 2001). Nevertheless, in recent years, the Environment Agency has done much to improve conditions for boat users. Its corporate plan for 2003/6 envisaged an increase in its navigation budget, and in 2004, it launched a campaign to encourage more pleasure boats to use the waterways it controls. This involved spending more than £400 million to improve moorings and other facilities in the river Thames, the Fens and the river Wye over the following ten years. 50 miles of new waterway would be opened to boats in East Anglia giving them access to a further 100 miles of waterway for their users to enjoy. These improvements were designed to benefit pleasure boating of all kinds, with priority to canoeing, rowing and sailing. The plans included new reaches for sailing and competition sites for canoeing and rowing. The agency claimed this would provide 'opportunities for everyone to enjoy our rivers' – everyone, of course, except swimmers (Environment Agency 2004: para. 4.2).

Sailers, canoeists and rowers may have had reason to feel that the agency has treated them as poor relations to the anglers. But their demands upon water space have at least been regarded as legitimate, even if a low priority, and recent spending plans will help to redress the balance. Not so for swimmers. The agency's corporate plan for 2003-6 said that promoting water-based recreation was a primary aim, with clean waters for 'those uses needed by a thriving and healthy community' (Environment Agency n.d.(b)). This aim was highlighted in the plan, and illustrated with a picture of two small children playing at the seaside. Swimming was mentioned only in the context of the Bathing Water Directive and coastal waters forgetting that we have a few inland bathing waters. There was nothing about improving inland waters for swimming. Since then the agency has recognised swimmers as legitimate users of inland waters – but this has not extended to practical help.

The role of the agency in relation to swimming has been essentially a negative one: erecting notices near weirs and other places where swimming is judged to be dangerous and generally discouraging swimming in all its rivers. It is important to warn people of any specific or unusual dangers but, given the agency's duty to promote the recreational use of water, one might expect that, where it is the riparian landowner, it would also seek to improve some of the relatively safe places where people swim now, or make suitable new sites available for swimming. The agency does not, on the whole, own land adjacent to the waterways it controls, but it does contribute to partnership projects that improve the environment and extend access to waterside areas for walkers, cyclists and horse riders – users who, like swimmers, do not bring in revenue. But such projects do not include making water available, or more suitable, for swimming.

It must be acknowledged, of course, that many water-based and waterside users, including those who swim in rivers, benefit indirectly from the Environment Agency's work in improving water quality and maintaining flows. The agency now defines its water quality objectives for rivers in relation to certain uses of the waters. Every classified stretch of river has its own River Quality Objectives which are based on the water quality needed to safeguard water supplies for domestic consumption, industry and agriculture as well as to protect the needs of fish and the use of the river for recreation. Similarly, the agency controls the abstraction of water from rivers in order to ensure that there is sufficient water for various needs and, in particular, to protect important wetland habitats. Levels of abstraction, to achieve sustainable use of water resources, are set out in Catchment Abstraction Management Strategies. These plans bring benefits to wildlife, the environment and, indirectly, for swimmers too, but they do not take into account the interests of swimming.

The Environment Agency also plays an important role in monitoring the water quality of 'bathing waters', in accordance with the Bathing Water Directive, and securing improvements where they fall below the standard. Since we have a few inland bathing waters, we look at the directive below. Elsewhere, until a recent change of heart, the agency has seen swimming in inland waters as a hazardous activity to be discouraged, a view shared by British Waterways and water companies.

British Waterways and the Canal and River Trust

British Waterways, a public corporation, was until recently responsible for managing 2,000 miles of navigable waterways in England, Scotland and Wales but, in 2012, its duties in England and Wales were transferred to a new charitable trust, the Canal and River Trust. It is too soon to know what changes this may bring but, initially, we can assume the policies and practice are likely to remain much the same. The waterways, mainly canals but including some rivers such as the Severn and Trent, have been maintained mainly for leisure. Canal building in Britain dates back to the Roman occupation, with some later works, but the heyday of construction began in the mid-seventeenth century. A century later the network extended to about 4,250 miles (Ingman 1993: 18). Canals soon lost out to railways, many fell into disrepair and those that remained might have been closed in the 1960s had it not been for their recreational value. The British Waterways Board, set up by the 1968 Transport Act, developed its waterways for recreation and amenity. Some still carry freight traffic, but they are managed mainly for people to enjoy cruising and fishing, and walking or cycling along the towpaths.

British Waterways was required to run its affairs, as far practicable, on a commercial basis – which limited its ability to spend money on non-profitable leisure uses.

Nevertheless it received considerable sums in public subsidy. Although its trading income increased steadily from under one-third of its total income in 1999/2000 to 45 per cent in 2003/04, the corporation received more than £109 million from public funds in that year. In addition to regular grants from government, this subsidy included 'third-party funding', often for expensive capital projects like canal restoration schemes, from sources such as the European Commission, the Heritage Lottery Fund, the Millennium Commission and development agencies. Although some of the corporation's income was derived from leisure-boat users, in terms of craft licences and mooring fees, and from anglers in terms of rod licences, this was relatively small – about £14,700 in 2003/04. This was a tiny fraction of its trading income (most of which came from other commercial sources, including property, wayleaves and premiums) and an even smaller fraction of the total public subsidy (see table 4.2). No figures were available to indicate what proportion of the corporation's budget benefited specific activities, but it seems clear that users of leisure boats have been the major beneficiaries, and the tow paths are enjoyed by many others, anglers and walkers, birdwatchers and cyclists (British Waterways 2004:74).

Table 4.2: British Waterways: income (£m)

Sources of income	2002/03	2003/04
Trading income	81.7	88.3
Restoration and third party funding	27.9	14.3
Government grant	82.0	94.8
Total revenue	191.6	197.4

Source: British Waterways 2004

British Waterways was the largest provider of recreational water space in the UK (Ingman 1993:23) – but not for swimmers who have been prohibited by the corporation's by-laws from enjoying its waterways. This blanket ban on swimming reflected the board's concern about the dangers for swimmers, including that of Weil's disease, as well as its desire not to inconvenience other canal users.[3] Canals certainly present hazards for swimmers, especially near locks and where there is considerable boat traffic. Those within an urban or industrial areas may tempt youngsters to jump in on a hot day, but offer little attraction for regular swimming. But the quality of the water in canals, though it varies considerably, has been steadily improving, and some canals have good water quality.[4] Some stretches that run through open country, such as sections of the Leeds-to-Liverpool canal within the Yorkshire Dales National Park, could offer attractive, and relatively safe, places to swim. The new Canal and River Trust has indicated that it will adopt a more flexible policy towards swimming so that such possibilities may, perhaps, become open to us.

The water companies

The main water companies in England and Wales own several hundred surface reservoirs. They are, therefore, in a better position to exercise direct control over the use of their waters than the Environment Agency which, although it owns some land, generally does not own the rights to use the rivers over which its policies operate. The water companies, though now privatised, have duties under the Water Act 1991 (Section 3-5) to promote recreational use of the land and water they manage. The act requires them to take such steps as are reasonably practicable and consistent with their other duties 'to ensure that water and land is made available, in the best manner, for recreational purposes'. Government advice to the companies reminds them that flooded gravel pits have great potential for water sports, walking and birdwatching; it urges them to promote 'access for everyone beside, to and on water', but does not mention swimming (DETR 2000 (a)).

Before the 1960s the water authorities, then responsible for water supplies, often prohibited public access to their lakes or the gathering grounds around them in order to safeguard the quality of water supplies. Now their successors, the water companies, who own the reservoirs and lakes as well as extensive areas of land around them, are increasingly inviting the public to enjoy them. They allow numerous activities on surface reservoirs and on the adjacent land.[5] Fishing, sailing, canoeing, sail-boarding, water-skiing and, in some cases, sub-aqua, are often allowed on or in the water, while opportunities for walking, picnicking, bird-watching, cycling, horse riding, even orienteering and climbing, are to be found on the land. Again we find that fishing is by far the most prevalent and favoured activity. Wessex Water, for example, allows sailing only where it would not interfere with fishing and explains, as one of the many reasons for not allowing swimming, that it would be unpopular with anglers and sailors.[6]

None of the main water companies in England and Wales allow informal swimming in their surface reservoirs. This is not because swimmers pollute the water; they consider their water purification processes can cope with that. It is, they say, simply a concern for the safety of swimmers. They emphasize that reservoirs are often deep and cold, with particular dangers near their outlets, and some experience algal blooms in summer. The only exceptions to the no-swimming policy have been occasional club events, such as triathlons in Rutland Water. Other water sports are allowed on some reservoirs: club-based sports where, the companies point out, club rules govern the behaviour of members and help to secure safety. A few companies have allowed sub aqua which, as we show in chapter 7, appears to be more dangerous than swimming. No water company is willing to allow even club-based swimming apart from Anglian Water which, as we see in the Postscript, will soon accommodate a swimming area in Rutland Water.

The European Commission

The European Commission has issued a number of directives designed to improve water quality and the environment, of which the most important for swimmers was the Bathing Water Directive (76/160/EEC). The original directive, applying to inland as well as coastal waters, was adopted by the Council of Ministers in December 1975. Whereas public policy in this country had been firmly opposed to helping people to swim in rivers and lakes, the directive was instrumental in bringing about significant improvements in water quality for coastal swimmers. But, as with many environmental improvements promoted by the European Union, it was implemented slowly by the United Kingdom government. The story of its implementation reflects a reluctance to invest in projects that protect the environment as well as a reluctance to take the interests of swimmers seriously – whether in the sea or inland.

The Bathing Water Directive set out two standards for water quality at bathing beaches: the 'mandatory' standard, with which member states were required to comply within ten years, and the much higher 'guideline' standard, which they should strive to achieve. The United Kingdom, initially operating through the publicly owned regional water boards and the former National Rivers Authority, was slow to respond to the letter, let alone the spirit, of the directive, ignoring the interests of the many coastal, as well as potentially inland, bathers.

Government guidance issued to the water boards (who at that time were responsible for testing the water) and to local authorities (who could seek to have their beaches included as bathing beaches) appears to have been designed to ensure that few stretches of water, where bathing took place, would qualify as 'bathing beaches'. An advice note issued by the Department of the Environment in 1980 explained that the directive defines 'bathing water' as fresh or sea water in which bathing is (a) explicitly authorised or (b) not prohibited and practised by a large number of bathers. The note stated, however, that 'explicitly authorised' would probably not be relevant to the UK. It went on to explain that, even if a beach displayed times at which public bathing was allowed there, if it had beach huts and life belts or even a lifeguard service, that did not mean bathing was 'explicitly authorised'. Even if you could pay to swim there, or if there were an artificially created pool that filled with sea water at high tide where you could swim, it did not mean that bathing was 'explicitly authorised'.[7] The note explained that, in terms of the second criterion, the Department of the Environment and the Welsh Office would not expect a stretch of water to be classified as bathing water unless there were at least 500 people in the water, though it failed to say how long this stretch of water needed to be. However, if there were more than 1,500 bathers per mile, then it would be classified as bathing water.[8]

As if that was not enough to deter them from designating bathing beaches, the water authorities were warned that, once a stretch of water was identified as a bathing beach, they would have to consider measures to bring the water up to standard (DOE 1980). And that, of course, was the crux of the problem: the investment that would then be needed to bring the country's aging sewage treatment and disposal systems up-to-date.

Even so, it is surprising that at first only 27 stretches of water were listed as 'bathing beaches' in the UK as a whole. Not even Blackpool was included. Table 4.3 shows how marked a contrast this was with other European countries. One would expect France and Italy, with their warmer summers and Mediterranean coastline, to identify many more bathing waters than the UK, but we see that Denmark identified 1,256 and the Netherlands 383. Even tiny landlocked Luxembourg identified 39 bathing waters (Jones1992: 37). Only Ireland was more reluctant to admit to having bathing beaches.

Table 4.3: Bathing waters identified under the Bathing Water Directive 1980

Member states	Inland waters	Coastal waters
Luxembourg	39	0
Belgium	41	15
Netherlands	323	60
Germany (FR)	85	9
Ireland	0	6
Denmark	139	1,117
France	1,362	1,498
Italy	57	3,308
United Kingdom	0	27

Source: Jones 1993: 37

By 1985 there were still only 27 designated bathing waters in the UK but, with pressures from the public, local authorities and environmental groups as well as threats of legal action from the European Commission, the list increased rapidly over the next five years to reach 446 by 1990 (Grantham 1992: 26). It continued to grow, and the criteria for designation also expanded to include other criteria such as access to the beach, toilets, car parks, lifeguards, first aid service, kiosk or shop, changing facilities and water sports facilities. Some much-loved quieter beaches, of course, do not get recognised. New bathing waters were identified where, following applications by local authorities, the government accepted that the beaches met some or all of the criteria.[9] By 2002 the Environment Agency was monitoring 478 designated bathing waters in England and Wales.

As the list expanded and the water companies invested in upgrading the aging sewerage infrastructure, the waters of our coastal bathing beaches gradually improved. In 1971 more than half the sewage outfalls on the coast were above low-water mark, pouring out smelly, unsightly and unhealthy discharges on to sea beaches – an issue that helped to mobilise the Marine Conservation Society and later Surfers Against Sewage. Of the 380 new bathing waters identified in 1987, 45 per cent failed to meet the mandatory, legally required, standard (Jones 1993: 35-39). Much progress has been made since then and, although the list of monitored sites increased, by 2011 nearly 98 per cent of designated bathing waters in England

and Wales complied with the minimum standard, and 88 per cent met the higher guideline standard. Sewage is still discharged on to some sea beaches, and storm water pipes discharge pollutants after heavy rain, so there is still some way to go.

It was not until 1998 that any inland bathing places were included in the list, and there are still only nine inland sites in England and Wales and eleven in the UK as a whole. In England and Wales we have three bathing areas on the shores of Lake Windermere, the three bathing ponds on Hampstead Heath, the Serpentine Lido in Hyde Park, part of Frensham Great Pond in Surrey and the beach at Cotswold Country Park in the Cotswold Water Park. They usually comply with the water quality standards of the Bathing Water Directive and sometimes meet the higher guideline standard. The children's beach at the Cotswold Country Park, a small part of a large flooded sand and gravel pit, has consistently met the higher standard at least since 2001. The London waters have more of a struggle. In 2010 the Hampstead Ponds only just managed to comply with the mandatory standard, having been given 'abnormal weather waivers' which mean that samples taken after a storm, that made the waters more dirty, were disregarded.

Table 4.4: Inland bathing waters in England and Wales: compliance with the Bathing Water Directive

Bathing place (England and Wales)	2010	2011
Beach, Cotswold Country Park	Guideline – pass	Guideline – pass
Ladies' Pond, Hampstead Heath	Mandatory – pass	Mandatory – pass
Men's Pond, Hampstead Heath	Mandatory – pass	Guideline – pass
Mixed Pond, Hampstead Heath	Mandatory – pass	Mandatory – pass
Serpentine, Hyde Park	Mandatory – pass	Mandatory – pass
Frensham Great Pond, Surrey	Guideline – pass	Guideline – pass
Lakeside YMCA, Lake Windermere	Guideline – pass	Guideline – pass
Millerground Landing, Lake Windermere	Guideline – pass	Guideline – pass
Fellfoot, Lake Windermere	Guideline – pass	Guideline – pass

Source: Environment Agency

Thus, after a slow start, we have made considerable progress in improving coastal bathing waters, but we still barely recognise swimming as a legitimate activity inland. In the 1999 bathing season there were 4,376 freshwater bathing waters in the European Union as a whole in contrast with just nine in England and Wales (European Commission 2000 (a)). This contrast probably reflects differences in attitude between the UK and other European countries towards bathing and in the legal framework relating to the ownership of land and access to water, as much as differences in public policy. In many member states the public has a right to use surface waters (rivers, lakes and sea) unless particular zones have been clearly prohibited (European Commission 2000 (b)). Bathing in lakes and rivers is widely practised.

In the Netherlands swimming takes place, and is regarded as acceptable, in most rivers, canals and lakes. It is usually forbidden only where there may be serious conflicts with wildlife or in particularly dangerous places such as in harbours. In Sweden people have a longstanding right of access to private land which, in the 1930s, was extended to enable everyone to enjoy outdoor activities, such as walking and bathing, almost everywhere (Segrell 1996: 148).

A revised Bathing Water Directive (76/1160/EEC) came into force in 2006 which sets more stringent water quality standards and puts a stronger emphasis on beach management and public information. It defines two main parameters for analysis (intestinal *enterococci* and *escherichia coli*) instead of nineteen in the previous directive. They are now used to monitor and assess the quality of bathing waters and to classify them. Other parameters could be taken into account, such as the presence of cyanobacteria or microalgae

It would clearly benefit swimmers if more inland sites were to be classified under the new directive. Not only would the Environment Agency then carry out regular checks on their water quality but also, where the waters do not come up to standard, seek to identify the sources of pollution and secure action to tackle the problem. But many informal swimming spots, including those used by swimming clubs, tend to be small scale and, unlike the seaside resorts, do not have a commercial interest in seeking designation as a bathing water. The Department for Environment, Food and Rural Affairs (DEFRA) now seeks suggestions from interested organisations for inland sites that might qualify for designation, but applications must come from a local authority, landowner or whoever controls the bathing water.[10] Even landowners who are happy to allow people to swim in their waters may fear that designation would result in onerous demands upon them if they failed to meet the standard, and some swimmers fear that monitoring might lead to a cessation of swimming. The managers of the Henleaze Swimming Club and the Farleigh Hungerford Club, which we look at in Chapter 9, were both reluctant to seek designation in 2011.

So, in the near future at least, the revised directive is unlikely to result in many more official inland bathing sites, nor the monitoring and consequent pressures for improvements to water quality that designation could bring. In the absence of designated sites swimming is not being taken into account in the river basin management plans that are being drawn up in response to the Water Framework Directive. If our countryside policy makers and land managers had regarded inland swimming as legitimate and desirable, there might have been pressure for sites to be designated as bathing waters. But, as we shall see in the next chapter, most of them have been as unwilling as the guardians of our water environment to consider the interests of swimmers.

5

A COUNTRYSIDE FOR ALL?

What is more pleasant than on a fine afternoon to take one's tea and go down to the river ... The children too, if it is hot enough, can paddle or even swim under the watchful eyes of their parents.

Patrick Abercrombie *Greater London Plan* (1944: 101)

It is generally advisable to actively discourage swimming in most inland waters.

RoSPA *Safety at Inland Waters Sites: Operational Guidelines* (1999: 48)

About a century after Her Majesty's Commissioners of Woods and Forests were creating Victoria Park for the enjoyment of the people of London's East End, town and country planners, under the direction of Sir Patrick Abercrombie, were drawing up plans to guide the development of London and its surroundings, plans that included the creation of new parks and the improvement of bathing places for Londoners to enjoy. The agencies that plan, and particularly those that own and manage land, have powers and responsibilities that affect the way we are able to use land and water for recreation. Here we examine the policies of the main players: the Countryside Commission and its successors, the Sports Council, the Forestry Commission, national park authorities and, most importantly, local authorities.

Countryside advisory bodies

The official advisory bodies on countryside policy – the former Countryside Commission, later the Countryside Agency and now English Nature, and the Countryside Council for Wales – have not only advised governments but also influenced the policies and projects carried out by local authorities and other organisations through the grants they give.[1]

In the 1970s the Countryside Commission, whose remit included England and Wales, championed country parks and contributed generously to their development. They were intended to enable people living in towns to enjoy countryside activities which, initially, included wild swimming. In later years the commission lost interest in swimming, though it continued to talk about 'a countryside for all'. By the 1990s it was worried about the competing pressures for water space and threats to the environment posed by power boats and other noisy sports, and promised to 'seek to improve public access to lakes, rivers and canals for informal recreation'. But it made no mention of swimming (Countryside Commission 1991(b): 6). Neither the Countryside Agency, which took over the commission's role in England, nor its successor English Nature, have any interest in swimming. The Countryside Council for Wales, however, recognises swimmers as legitimate users of inland waters, as I explain in the Postscript, and is consulting on codes of conduct for angling, canoeing and wild swimming.

The Sports Councils

The sports councils, whose status have also changed, have been primarily concerned, of course, with competitive sports, but they have also extended their help to less competitive activities. The former Sports Council, an advisory and grant-giving body established in 1972, had a responsibility, among other duties, to encourage sporting activities in the English countryside. It defined 'countryside sports' as those sports and recreational activities based primarily on the natural resources of the countryside: land, air and water. In consulting other organisations on what its policies should be, the council listed 29 possible countryside sports. These ranged from minority activities such as ballooning and parachuting to popular ones such as rambling and cycling, but they did not include swimming (Sports Council 1990: 5). The subsequent policy statement pledged support to a wide range of outdoor sports, including risky sports such as rock climbing and white-water canoeing, as well as more traditional activities such as rambling and horse riding. It proclaimed its mission as 'Sport for All' – again, for all except swimmers, of whom there was no mention (Sports Council 1992).

The Regional Councils for Sport and Recreation (RCSR), set up in 1976, had the task of translating such policies into action through regional recreational strategies. They displayed a more promotional attitude towards active recreation in the countryside than the Countryside Commission, championing the demands of the newly developing water sports. The strategy for water recreation in part of the Eastern Region, for example, pointed out that the large expanses of enclosed waters being created by mineral extraction in this area would be suitable for water-based recreation. It described each complex of lakes and its potential, mentioning in addition to the active water sports other non-competitive pastimes such as walking. But again there was no mention of swimming (ECSR 1989).

The Forestry Commission

Whereas the countryside agencies and the sports councils are essentially policy-making bodies, operating indirectly through advice and grants to other agencies, the Forestry Commission, whose responsibilities extend throughout Great Britain, not only gives advice and grants but is also a major landowner. Thus it can exercise more direct control over the way in which its land and water are used.

As the economic justification for timber production has declined over recent years, the commission has played an increasingly active role in providing opportunities for people to enjoy its forests. The 1967 Forest Act gave the commission powers to develop recreation facilities in its own forests and to encourage such provision in private forests. Although the Forestry Commission's work and the recreational opportunities it provides focus on forested land, some forest parks have lakes within them or rivers flowing through them. The commission does not appear to have a overall policy on swimming but, in practice, seems to be more accommodating than other agencies.[2] Certainly there are attractive spots within Forestry Commission land where people swim without apparent restrictions. These include the gently flowing river Thet, on its way through the Thetford Forest, and the much more bracing waterfall pools of the river Nedd above Pontneddfechan in South Wales. Indeed, in the Nedd Valley it is fishing and canoeing, not swimming, that is forbidden.

There are also lakes within the forests where swimming is allowed or, at least, not obviously banned. Some lakes within Forestry Commission land are owned or managed by water companies and therefore subject to the water companies' ban on bathing in surface reservoirs, such as Lake Kielder in Northumberland and Llyn Brenig in North Wales. However, swimming takes place in Llyn Geirionydd, a delightful small lake in the wooded hilly countryside of North Wales, within Forestry Commission land (see box 'A Jewel in the Welsh Hills'). Here the head of the lake is reserved for non-motorised water sports and although swimming is informal and unsupervised, according to a Forestry Commission spokesman, it has not given rise to any problems.[3]

National park authorities

National parks in England and Wales were set up, under the 1949 National Parks and Access to the Countryside Act, to protect areas of scenic beauty and provide opportunities for people to enjoy them. They are governed by national park authorities (NPAs) comprising representatives of the constituent local authorities and members appointed by government. In contrast to many other countries, the land within national parks in this country is largely in private ownership, with the Forestry Commission and the National Trust each owning about 7 per cent, and the national park authorities only 2.3 per cent. Thus the way that the Forestry Commission and the National Trust manage their properties is more significant for swimmers than the policies of the NPAs.

The NPAs are seldom in a position either to allow or to forbid bathing, but they can introduce by-laws, subject to government approval, which can be used to protect swimmers or to make conditions better for swimming. The by-law imposing a 10mph restriction on boats on Lake Windermere, for example, designed to protect the enjoyment of many other quiet users of the lake and the land around, also makes swimming more enjoyable. The Friends of Llyn Geirionydd, as we see in the box on page 46, were unsuccessful in persuading the Snowdonia National Park Authority to introduce a similar by-law. This is not surprising as the legal proce-

A JEWEL IN THE WELSH HILLS

The land rises steeply from the Conway Valley to form the eastern edge of Snowdonia National Park. This is a land of hills and wood and lakes, with clearings and boggy patches, remnants of lead mine workings and monuments to past heroes – a small-scale and more intimate landscape than the better-known mountains further west.

Within this delightful countryside lies Llyn Geirionydd, a small lake partly owned by the Forestry Commission. Near the head of the lake, where the commission has provided a car park, picnic area and lavatories, an area is marked off by buoys and here people can canoe, windsurf and swim. When so many lakes in Wales are water-supply reservoirs in which bathing is banned, it is a welcome surprise to find one in which to swim.

Part of the lakeshore is owned by a water-ski club, giving its members rights to use the lake for jet-skiing and water-skiing. The club limits the number of boats that can use the lake at the same time, but other users of the lake and the land around feel that the noise interferes with their enjoyment. They argue that such sports are inappropriate in a national park. Friends of Llyn Geirionydd have campaigned to persuade the Snowdonia National Park Authority to introduce a by-law, similar to that on Lake Windermere, for a 10mph speed limit on the lake. In 2003 they delivered a petition to the authority, with 789 signatures, pressing for such action. After commissioning studies into the use of the lake and the impact of motorised craft on noise levels and water pollution, the authority decided the nuisance did not justify enacting a by-law, but promised to continue to survey and test the lake and, if necessary, review the matter in future years. No such review appears to have been undertaken.[4]

Many people visit the countryside principally to find 'peace and quiet'. [5] The principle of 'quiet enjoyment' was until recently enshrined as one of the twin purposes of a national park but, unfortunately, this significant phrase was omitted from the 1995 Environment Act. Water-skiers are now seeking more opportunities to use lakes in national parks, especially the larger lakes of the Lake District. Let's hope that such pressures are successfully resisted and that, in this little lake, peace will one day be restored.

dures required for the enactment of such by-laws are long and costly, involving extensive consultations and take many years to complete.

People exploring our upland national parks, however, have relatively good access to rivers, lakes and tarns in which they can often swim, in practice if not by right. In the Lake District National Park there is usually nothing to stop walkers bathing in upland tarns on unenclosed land. Snowdonia and Dartmoor, too, offer many spots where one can swim, informally, in lakes, pools or rivers. Much of the freedom in national parks appears to derive from a more *laissez-faire* attitude on the part of land owners, including the National Trust and the Forestry Commission, in the uplands and unenclosed land. Swimmers may have no legal right to swim and in some places swimming may be officially prohibited but, in practice, tolerated. The National Trust owns some of the most attractive parts of the Lake District National Park including two out of the three official bathing sites on Lake Windermere (which are featured later in the box on page 113). Elsewhere, the trust normally does not allow swimming in waters within its properties, but it does not indicate this beside lakes in open country nor take any action to stop swimming in them.[6]

In contrast the Broads, technically not a national park but having equivalent status, give few opportunities for swimming. The Broads, covering part of Norfolk and Suffolk, is the largest protected wetland in Britain, with rivers, shallow lakes, marshes and fen, provide for a wide range of activities which, the authority claims, are compatible with its importance for wildlife. These include sailing, canoeing, fishing, birdwatching and walking. They also include more disruptive activities, such as motor-cruising and water-skiing, despite the park authority's aims to protect wildlife: a contradiction to which we will return in chapter 11. Specific areas are demarcated for water-skiing, but none for swimming. Bathing, though not officially banned, is not encouraged anywhere in the Broads. The management explains that this is to protect the health and safety of swimmers from the dangers posed by boat traffic, aquatic vegetation and the frequent blooms of blue-green algae which are a particular problem in these eutrophic waters in the summer.[7]

The role of local authorities

Local authorities can extend or restrict the opportunities to swim in several ways. Firstly, they can introduce by-laws, subject to the approval by government, to control the use of water. By-laws can be used to restrict bathing where it is considered dangerous, or to restrict other activities that might interfere with, or endanger, bathers. In practice, they are normally used to restrict bathing rather than to protect bathers.

Secondly local authorities can, through their strategic planning functions, determine whether land can be developed and broadly for what sort of use, and through their development-control powers they have more detailed control over how land is developed. In allocating land for open space and recreational use, local authorities can influence whether good swimming sites are protected. But, except where they own the land, the degree to which they can determine precisely how sites or water bodies are used thereafter is limited. Local authorities could, through their control over the excavation of land for minerals, ensure that land is restored in such a way that the lakes thereby created offer potential for water sports and are suitable for swimming. Such possibilities are discussed in chapter 12. But again, unless the local authority is prepared to buy the land, it cannot ensure that swimming is allowed.

Thirdly, and potentially much more important, local authorities can decide whether or not people will be allowed to swim in lakes or rivers within sites that they own and manage. It is through their ownership and management of country parks that local authorities have exercised their most direct control over opportunities to enjoy land and water for recreation. We discuss this below. Before that, however, we look at three more extensive areas where local authorities have worked together to create large regional parks to enable people to enjoy outdoor sporting and leisure activities – areas in which one might expect there to be some places where people could swim.

Regional parks

Sir Patrick Abercrombie certainly had swimming in mind when he sketched plans for an extensive linear park, to be created after the Second World War, as a playground for the overcrowded East End of London. The park would be developed in an area that included 24 miles of waterways, marshes, derelict industrial land, sewage works, old mineral workings and open spaces. Abercrombie recognised that the old gravel pits offered a magnificent opportunity to create places of beauty where people could enjoy boating and bathing (Abercrombie 1945: 106).

In large part this ambitious plan was realised. The Lee Valley Regional Park, created in 1966 by an Act of Parliament sponsored by three county councils (London, Hertfordshire and Essex) and now managed by the Lee Valley Regional Park Authority, extends from near the Thames in Limehouse to Ware in Hertfordshire. Forty different sports are now catered for in the park, including many water sports in the waterways and flooded gravel workings. But by-laws forbid informal bathing in all the lakes. The only exceptions are the usual ones, such as scuba diving or triathlon training, which are sometimes allowed in designated areas of one of the gravel pits. It is not clear whether the idea of using gravel pits for outdoor bathing was simply forgotten, or deliberately abandoned, in subsequent plans for the park. A park manager, searching through the archives, could find no explicit explanation of why swimming dropped out of the plans but suggested that the reasons related to contamination of the water by hazardous infill material leaching into some of the flooded gravel pits, under-water obstructions such as old greenhouses and cars, the dangers of Weil's disease and a lack of demand.[8]

The Colne Valley Regional Park presents a similar story. It was set up in the 1960s as a partnership between local authorities, government agencies, private companies, local voluntary groups and the environmental charity Groundwork Thames Valley. The park stretches across parts of three counties, Buckinghamshire, Hertfordshire and Surrey, and several lower-tier authorities, forming the first significant area of countryside to the west of London. Much of the land is in private ownership but it contains country parks owned by local authorities, and an extensive network of public paths. It is a mosaic of farmland, woods and water, extending over 43 square miles, and includes 50 miles of river and canal and more than 40 lakes, mostly formed from the extraction of gravel. People can enjoy sailing, canoeing, windsurfing, water skiing, and model boating, but not open-water swimming on any of the waters within the park.[9]

The Cotswold Water Park, in the upper reaches of the Thames Valley, is another coop-erative venture by local authorities designed to provide recreational facilities on a large scale – in this case firmly focused on water sports. It was designated in 1967 and covers a extensive area where gravel extraction had been going on since the 1920s. Many of the worked-out pits had been left as wet pits and were colonised by a wide variety of wildlife. A master plan, approved in 1970, sought to resolve the conflicts between continuing gravel extraction with its associated traffic, the environment for people living in the villages within the park, its visitors and its wildlife. The local authorities controlled the restoration of the extraction sites to make sure they were left suitable for recreational use. They required trees to be retained, the shorelines of lakes to be graded and the surrounding land to be landscaped. By 2012 the park covered 40 square miles and includes 150 lakes, almost entirely in private ownership. Many different water sports can be enjoyed here, as well as picnicking, cycling and horse riding. The water quality in the lakes is generally very good and, not surprising, the first FAQ on the park's website is 'Where is the beach?' Apart from triathlon sessions at one lake, and a short Saturday morning swimming session at another, the only place where you can casually paddle and swim is in one small corner of a lake at the Cotswold Country Park.

Country parks

Although about one-third of the land within the Lee Valley Regional Park is publicly owned, much of the land in the Colne Valley and the Cotswold Water Park, like the land within national parks, is in private ownership, so that although the authorities can control or prevent certain activities taking place, their ability to ensure that particular activities are allowed is limited. Even if the park managers considered that swimming was desirable, they could not ensure that it would be allowed. Most country parks, however, are owned and managed by local authorities who therefore have direct control. Thus one might expect to find opportunities for swimming in country parks, particularly as the original legislation envisaged that bathing would be one of the activities to be found in them.

The 1968 Countryside Act provided for the creation of country parks and picnic sites, and empowered the newly created Countryside Commission to give 75 per cent grants for this purpose. To qualify for a grant the park had to be equipped with car parks, visitor centres and a wardening service. The local authorities embraced the concept of country parks with far more enthusiasm than they put into extending access to the wider countryside. Nearly 300 such parks were created, mostly in the early 1970s by local authorities, but occasionally by private landowners. Many occupied not very attractive land to which the public already had informal *de facto* access (Shoard 1997). Now, however, as formal country parks, the activities within them could become more controlled.

The 1968 Countryside Act stated, under section 8, that 'where a country park comprises any waterway, the kinds of open-air recreation for which the local plan-ning authority concerned may provide facilities shall include sailing, boating, bathing and fishing'. This was repeated in the Countryside Commission's policy guidance (Countryside Commission 1972: 2). Many country parks included riversides, lakes or flooded former mineral workings and, over the years, have come to provide for many different activities including an increasing range of water sports. Country parks have been commended for the way that they have responded to the demand for water sports, but commentators fail to mention that few parks allow bathing.

In 2002 the Countryside Agency commissioned the Urban Parks Forum to survey the country parks in England, estimated at more than 270, as part of its policy review. This revealed that swimming was available in only 7 per cent of parks from which responses were received (Countryside Agency 2003). Again, as table 5.1 demonstrates, it is fishing that is the favoured activity. The forum's report did not explore the question of swimming further. However, analysis of the data collected for the review showed that, typically, it is the seaside parks where swimming is possible. Of 132 parks for which data were available, 65 contained lakes, 41 had riverside areas and 10 were on the coast.[10] Bathing was available at eight of the coastal parks, but in none of those with riversides. Of the 65 parks with lakes only two allowed bathing, and this was discontinued in one of them, Black Park Country Park, a few months later.

Table 5.1: Water-based activities in country parks in England 2002

Activity available	Percentage of parks
Angling	54
Boating	19
Sailing	18
Swimming	7
Waterskiing/Power boating	4
Source: Countryside Agency 2003	

Instead of enabling more people to swim in lakes and rivers, the creation of country parks had the opposite effect. In some parks swimming used to take place unofficially, but was discontinued when the park was formalised. In Milton Pits Country Park near Cambridge, for example, people used to swim in one of the lakes, but this was stopped owing to concern about underwater obstructions. At Brereton Country Park, as we see in the box on page 57, after the area became a country park, the council tried hard to stop people swimming but many continued to do so. In other cases, swimming was sanctioned at first but discontinued later. People had enjoyed swimming in the clear waters of the lake at Black Park Country Park for many decades before it became an official country park, and continued to do so after designation until it was banned in 2002 (see box 'No More Bathing in Black Park'). Now, although local authorities still occasionally create country parks, usually in partnership with other organisations, they are unlikely to allocate areas for swimming. One exception was Whitlingham Country Park, a recently developed park near Norwich which had a beach for paddling and a limited swimming area, but swimming was stopped a few years ago pending an investigation into an accidental

---

NO MORE BATHING IN BLACK PARK

'I think I was happiest in securing for the town the restoration of Black Park, an Eden of acres of beech trees and pines and a tree bordered lake' wrote Fenner Brockway of his years as MP for Eton and Slough (Brockway 1977: 156). The people of Slough were grateful for his efforts, particularly as the Ministry of Defence had taken over the site during the war and were using it as an ammunitions dump. Black Park Country Park, an attractive area of wooded heath just outside Slough, is part of a larger area of land that was bought by the local authorities (London County Council, Buckinghamshire County Council and Slough and Eton Borough Council) just after the war for public enjoyment. Its future seemed assured.

The park has a large tree-fringed artificial lake with clear waters that have filtered through the glacial sands and gravel that overlie the London clay. Its edges are shallow although the middle is deep and cold. Swimmers had enjoyed bathing in this lake for many decades, long before it became an official country park but, in 2002, Buckinghamshire County Council decided to ban swimming rather than meet the cost of providing the level of supervision advised by the Health and Safety Executive.

The ban met with angry protests. The Free Black Park Campaign was set up by a group of local mothers who, like generations before them, had taken their children to bathe at their 'local beach'.[12] Three years later the campaign continues. Unfortunately Fenner Brockway is no longer around to help, and the local mothers lack the money and legal connections that are helping the swimmers of Hampstead Heath in their campaign (see box on page 59).

Country parks were originally intended to enable people living in towns to enjoy countryside activities such as bathing near their homes. But, as with others, its designation as an official country park led to the loss of the long-standing freedom to swim. Had this 'local beach' been at the seaside, swimming would have continued regardless of whether the council could afford lifeguards. For some parents this is their seaside and they cannot afford to take their children further. Now they may wander along the pleasant perimeter path with tantalising views of this delightful lake and picnic overlooking the water. They may let their dogs swim, but not their children.

---

drowning. Here too swimming is no longer allowed.[11]

There are a few exceptions, two of which are particularly popular. In the Cotswold Country Park within the Cotswold Water Park, which we look at in chapter 9, bathing is allowed in one small corner of a larger lake. The area is so restricted, and the water so shallow, that it is not much more than a large children's paddling pool. At Frensham Great Pond, featured in the box on page 104, a more generous area is allocated for bathing.

Why no swimming?

A number of factors deter local authorities and other site operators from providing for, or simply allowing, swimming in lakes and rivers under their control. When the first country parks were being developed there were sometimes concerns about water quality and a reluctance to spend money on the site works, such as removing underwater obstructions or re-profiling lake margins, that might have been needed to make a lake suitable for bathing. At Kingsbury Water Park, for example, the managers were understandably unwilling to allow bathing or paddling, as the waters were downstream from a sewage works and in the flood plain of the river Tame which sometimes overflowed its banks.[13] In more recent years it has been shortage of money as spending on country parks generally did not keep pace with inflation (Countryside Agency 2003: 50). The costs of maintenance, particularly the cost of providing lifeguards which safety organisations began to insist upon, then became a major factor in determining whether local authorities would allow swimming. The decision by Buckinghamshire County Council to prohibit swimming at Black Park Country Park was made, reluctantly according to the council, because it could not afford to employ the 'statutory required number of lifeguards'. The council explained that extensive discussions had taken place with the Health and Safety Executive and the Royal Society for the Prevention of Accidents, but there was no room for compromise.[14] It feared that, were it to allow swimming to continue without lifeguards and an accident occurred, it might be prosecuted by the Health and Safety Executive.

Since country parks were first envisaged in the 1970s, local councils and other landowners, in addition to fearing prosecution, have become increasingly fearful that, if they allow people to swim at their own risk, they might be sued for damages if someone were injured or drowned. This fear of litigation under civil law, and the possible costs involved, persists even though legal rulings in 2003 should now allay such fear. There have also been, even more recently, important changes in the guidance given by both the Health and Safety Executive and the Royal Society for Accidents, that could enable landowners to consider allowing people to swim in their waters. We look at these issues in the next chapter.

6

LITIGATION OR LIBERTY?

Any operator considering designating a water zone for swimming, should be aware of the onerous responsibilities this entails to ensure all duties are met, and all risks adequately controlled.

RoSPA 1999: Appendix 7

Does the law require that all trees be cut down because some youths may climb them and fall? ... Does the law require that attractive picnic spots be destroyed because of a few foolhardy individuals who choose to ignore warning notices and indulge in activities dangerous only to themselves?

Lord Hobhouse in *Tomlinson v. Congleton Borough Council* 2003: para. 81

We have seen that British Waterways and the water companies have forbidden us to swim in the waters they control. The Environment Agency has, until very recently, discouraged us from swimming in lakes and rivers. In country parks, set up to enable people to enjoy quiet countryside pursuits, swimming is now mostly forbidden. The overt reason for this stance by public bodies is concern for the safety of swimmers. Safety warnings issue regularly from the fire and rescue services; the water companies stress the dangers of swimming in deep cold lakes; and safety figures prominently among the reasons given for banning swimming in country parks. But underlying these concerns for safety are cogent, probably more cogent, financial considerations – considerations that spring from the legal requirements of the duty of care and the way in which they have been interpreted. We look at these issues in this chapter.

Financial concerns

Whereas club-based sports, such as angling, sailing or subaqua, can generate revenue for riparian landowners, public and private, informal swimming generally does not. The Environment Agency and other controllers of water space collect some revenue from angling and boating licences though, as we saw in chapter 4, this does not cover the expenditure on these activities.

Informal swimming is more like walking and cycling, picnicking or birdwatching, activities which do not normally bring in revenue. The Environment Agency, British Waterways, water companies and local authorities have all welcomed such activities and spent money on them, providing paths and bridges, picnic tables and bird hides. Local authorities, in their country parks, have provided car parks, sometimes free of charge, lavatories, costly visitor centres, and employed wardens to look after the site: expenditure that could benefit any visitor. However, site operators wishing to allow swimming in their lakes have, in recent years, felt obliged to incur additional expenditure on lifeguards to satisfy the requirements of the duty of care, even on cool days when few people may be swimming. At a time of cutbacks in spending on their discretionary activities, such as maintaining country parks, it is understandable that supervised swimming has been seen as an area in which they could make savings.

The duty of care under civil law

Occupiers of land have long had a common-law 'duty of care' to take reasonable precautions to ensure the safety of their visitors, but this duty has been codified by legislation in the Occupiers' Liability Acts of 1957 and 1984.

The Occupiers' Liability Act 1957 set out the duty of care in relation to anyone coming onto the land or premises with an occupier's permission. It enacted rules 'to regulate the duty which an occupier of premises owes to his visitors in respect of dangers due to the state of the premises or to things done or omitted to be done on them' (section 1 (1)). Section 2 (2) requires the occupier to take such care as 'in all the circumstances of the case is reasonable to see that the visitor will be reasonably safe in using the premises for the purposes for which he is invited or permitted by the occupier to be there'. In order to carry out this duty, as section 2 (4) explains, the occupier must warn visitors of any danger and this warning must be sufficiently strong to enable the visitor to be reasonably safe. However, section 2 (5) makes it clear that this duty of care does not impose upon the occupier an obligation in respect of risks willingly accepted by the visitor. The act leaves open to interpretation the degree of care required to be taken. An occupier would not be liable for an injury resulting from a risk willingly undertaken by an adult visitor, but this might not be the case with young children, whose apparent 'willingness' may be uninformed by the possible dangers.[1]

The Occupiers' Liability Act 1984 extended the duty of care to trespassers, people who have not been invited or given permission to come onto the land or water, where the occupier is both aware of the dangers and also aware that people may come onto the land. Again, this duty of care may be discharged by taking such steps as are reasonable to give warning of the danger. It applies, however, only in situations where it is reasonable and practicable for the occupier to offer such protection. Thus, whereas a notice saying that people who swim do so at their own risk may be effective in the open countryside, it may not be adequate if there are unexpected risks or if the owner is charging for access to the water.[2]

The duty of care under criminal law

The Health and Safety at Work (HSAW) Act 1974, which relates to premises and sites where people are employed, also has implications for country parks and other sites where people might swim. If people are employed to manage a recreation site, then the activities on that site are considered to be 'work-related' under the act. Employers not only have a duty to ensure the safety of their employees, but they (and any self-employed people working on the premises) also have a duty of care to visitors to the site. Section 3 (1) states that 'It shall be the duty of every employer to conduct his undertaking in such a way as to ensure, so far as is reasonably practicable, that persons not in his employment who may be affected thereby are thereby not exposed to risks to their health or safety'. Contravention of this section is a criminal offence. This duty, which has even been seen as applying to farmers who allow the public to swim in rivers or ponds on their land, has been a major concern to operators of sites designed for public recreation.

Advice by safety watchdogs

The interpretation of the legislation relating to the duty of care under both civil and criminal legislation, and the advice given to site operators by the Health and Safety Executive (HSE), the official body responsible for regulating and enforcing the HWSA Act, and the Royal Society for the Prevention of Accidents (RoSPA), the influential safety charity, have been major deterrents to councils that might consider allowing swimming in their parks.

The HSE has, until recently, advised local authorities that they need either to discourage swimming or to follow its guidelines on the management of swimming pools (HSG179). The blue book, as it is usually called, was drawn up with conventional swimming pools in mind, and provides comprehensive advice on their safety management. It also has 'limited application to pools which consist of segregated areas of rivers, lakes and the sea' but gives no explicit consideration to them (HSE/Sport England 2003: 2). The blue book's guidance on the number of lifeguards needed at a pool has, however, been applied to open waters. It suggests a minimum of one lifeguard (or two at busy times) for a small pool of 20m by 8.5m, increasing to four (or six at busy times) for a pool of 50m by 20m. Although these numbers are only indicative – they do not contain the word 'must' which would give them legal status – and although they are based on conventional swimming pools, some inspectors have treated them as mandatory for lakes in country parks. One inspector explained, after the decision to ban swimming in Black Park Lake, that such a lake 'is little different from an open air pool' so that unless swimming is effectively discouraged, the 'constant supervision of sufficient qualified lifeguards is necessary'.[3] The executive has now clarified the scope of the blue book to make it clear that its recommendations no longer apply to open waters where swimming is simply allowed, rather than actively encouraged. But the fear of being prosecuted by the executive lingers on.

It is RoSPA, perhaps, that bears more responsibility for the proliferation of no-swimming rules. Its advice has, until very recently, been more stringent and explicit than advice from the HSE. RoSPA's guidelines for inland water sites, which it issued in 1999, outlined measures to improve the safety of other water sports, but for swimming its message was simple: prohibit and enforce. It described how water-sides could be modified to inhibit swimming by, for example, planting prickly bushes in front of gently shelving edges. It advised that swimming should be discouraged in most inland waters and that site operators should enforce 'no swim-ming' rules to ensure that people who might be tempted to swim were prevented from doing so. 'Where swimming has traditionally taken place ... and an assessment indicates it to be a high risk, then special wardens may also be needed to prevent the activity on hot days – particularly during school holidays' (RoSPA 1999: 48).

RoSPA's guidelines did acknowledge that there could be 'designated locations with optimal conditions, and formal supervision systems, where programmed swimming may take place with relatively low risk', but warned anyone considering whether to allow swimming of the 'onerous responsibilities' that this entailed (RoSPA 1999: Appendix 7). They warned that unless managers could control all the risks they could face claims for negligence. Even in cases where there has been no obvious negligence, 'councils may be advised to settle out of court because of the high legal costs and the costs of officer time which may not be recovered, even if the case is won' (Baylis et al. 1995: 1).

In these circumstances it is understandable that hard-pressed local authorities, concerned to maintain core services, have chosen to ban swimming in the lakes for which they have responsibility rather than provide lifeguards, even at traditional popular swimming spots with a good safety record where people want to continue to swim. Or, where occasionally they do allow swimming, they may confine it to one small corner that is easy to supervise.

A changing legal landscape

Recent legal decisions in relation to both civil and criminal liability make it clear that safety organisations have been interpreting their duty of care too onerously. RoSPA, as I explain in the Postscript, is reviewing its stance, for its advice to site operators that they must stop people from swimming where 'no swimming' rules are in force, went beyond the legal requirements.

In one civil case, damages had been awarded against the National Trust to a woman whose husband had drowned while swimming in a lake which it owned. Swimming was forbidden in the lake, but there was only an inconspicuous sign in the car park to this effect and, though wardens would warn people from time to time that they might catch Weil's disease if they swam, there were no systematic attempts to stop people from doing so. In allowing an appeal by the National Trust, the Court of Appeal ruled that there was no need to display warning signs next to the lake, as it did not present any unusual risk. Lord Justice May pointed out that, had the appeal been dismissed, warning notices would have to be put up beside

CARING COUNCIL OR CORPORATE VANDAL?

Many country parks were developed on semi-derelict land, sometimes former gravel workings or quarry sites with flooded pits, which were already used by people for recreation. In this respect Brereton Country Park in Cheshire is not unusual. After quarrying ceased in the 1970s people enjoyed picnicking, partying and swimming in the lake. Congleton Borough Council bought the land in 1980, turned it into a country park and began to discourage swimming. Warning notices were put up but were ignored. The park, though owned by the borough council, was managed by Cheshire County Council. In 1990 the county council's water safety officer recommended that reeds be planted to deter swimmers. He went on to advise that swimming in lakes, rivers and ponds be discouraged at all the county council's sites, suggesting that people might be deterred by warnings of Weil's disease and blue-green algae. If this failed, he argued, ballast should be dumped on beaches, banks made muddy and unattractive, and reeds and shrubs planted.

At Brereton the warnings were ineffective and many people continued to swim. Several near-drowning incidents were reported, often associated with high-spirited, sometimes drunken, youths playing around in the water. But families also continued to enjoy the area for picnicking, paddling and swimming. Though 160,000 people visited the park every year, and as many as 200 would be bathing on a fine summer's day, no one had drowned since it had opened in 1982.

The borough council, fearing it might be liable for damages were an accident to occur, decided to block the entrance and destroy the beach. But before this work was completed a young man dived in shallow water, hit his head on the sandy bottom and suffered injuries which left him severely disabled. The council's fears appeared to be well-founded, as he was awarded partial damages by the Court of Appeal. This ruling, however, was overturned by the House of Lords.

It was hard on the injured young man, but a significant victory for swimmers. More important, it was a stand against the excessive caution urged by organisations like RoSPA and fears of litigation that restrict the freedom of people to enjoy themselves without causing harm to others. As Lord Hobhouse stressed: 'the law does not require disproportionate and unreasonable responses' (*Tomlinson v. Congleton Borough Council 2003*: para. 45).

every beach in the country (*Darby v. National Trust* 2001).

In another case, a young man was injured when he dived in shallow water in the lake at Brereton Heath Country Park (see box 'Caring Council or Corporate Vandal?'). The country park was owned by Congleton Borough Council, but managed by Cheshire County Council. Swimming in the lake was forbidden, and not only were there warning notices in place but the borough council had been planning to block the entrance to the lake and had even begun to destroy a popular beach to prevent people from swimming there. The Court of Appeal awarded the young man (Tomlinson) partial damages, but the case was taken to the House of Lords which upheld an appeal by the councils. In doing so the Law Lords made it clear that landowners are not under a duty to take steps to prohibit or prevent people from swimming in open water where there is no unusual danger over and above that of swimming in the water. In Lord Hoffmann's words: 'it will be extremely rare for an occupier of land to be under a duty to prevent people from taking risks which are inherent in activities they freely choose to undertake on the land'. (Tomlinson v. Congleton Borough Council 2003: para. 45)

The judgement in the Brereton Country Park case, as in the National Trust case, related to a site where swimming was not allowed by the site operator. But it would appear from the reasoning that accompanied the House of Lords' decision that the ruling may have wider application. The Law Lords, in their judgement, agreed that the duties of care under the Occupiers' Liability Act 1957, where visitors are permitted to be on the premises, are broadly the same as those under the 1984 Act, which applies to trespassers – indeed there was some disagreement among the Lords about whether, in diving rather than swimming, the injured young man was a trespasser or not. Lord Hoffmann emphasised that a landowner might wish, for his own reasons, to prohibit certain activities on his land, but the law did not require him to do so. It would seem that where landowners know that swimming takes place but do not try to prevent it, they would be complying with the requirements of section 1 (5) of the Occupiers' Liability Act 1984 provided that they warn people of any unusual dangers (dangers arising from the nature of the site rather than the dangers inherent in the activity) and provided that the danger does not arise from things done or omitted to be done by the landowner.

The Law Lords stated that the Court of Appeal had ignored two important issues: the social value of the activities that might otherwise be prohibited and the freedom of adults to decide for themselves whether to take a risk. Lord Hoffmann considered that the Court of Appeal, in awarding partial damages to Tomlinson, had failed to give proper regard to the social value of activities connected with the lake. In alluding to Congleton Borough Council's actions in destroying the popular bathing beach, Lord Hobhouse commented that the arguments put forward on Tomlinson's behalf 'attack the liberty of the individual to engage in dangerous, but otherwise harmless, pastimes at his own risk and the liberty of citizens as a whole fully to enjoy the variety and quality of the landscape of this country' (Tomlinson v. Congleton Borough Council 2003: para. 81).

The two decisions referred to did not, however, address the question of liability under section 3 (1) of the HSAW Act which requires employers to ensure, so far as is reasonably practicable, that visitors to the site are not exposed to risks to their health or safety. The application of the HSAW Act was not relevant to those civil law proceedings. Although, in the view of an HSE spokesperson, it is the fear of civil litigation that tends to be the major deterrent to operators,[4] concern about duties

A SWIM BEFORE WORK?

Passions were running high among Hampstead swimmers in the autumn of 2003. *The Camden New Journal* reported that on 2 October a policeman and dog patrolled outside the hall where 70 angry swimmers quizzed the Corporation of London's legal consultants on winter swimming.

Bathers had enjoyed dawn-to-dusk swimming in all three ponds on Hampstead Heath for over a century. The Men's Pond and the Ladies' Pond stayed open all year but, earlier in 2003, the corporation announced plans to open later on winter mornings. The plan, ostensibly to meet safety concerns, provoked bitter opposition among regular swimmers, some of whom would no longer be able to swim before going to work. The United Swimmers' Association (USA), on behalf of the swimmers, asked the corporation to allow members of a specially formed club to swim in the Mixed Pond, unsupervised and at their own risk, when closed to the public in winter. Consultants for the Amateur Swimming Association advised against this idea, arguing that it would not absolve the corporation of liability for accidents, and recommended even more restricted opening hours.

The USA also sought legal advice which, in contrast, concluded that the corporation would not face a risk under the duty of care provided that (a) proper steps had been taken to ensure that self-regulated swimmers were identified and organised, and (b) the swimmers acknowledged that they understood and accepted the risks of such swimming.[7] The USA's counsel explained that there was nothing in the ordinary conditions that a winter swimmer might encounter in the pond that would constitute a defect in the 'state of the premises' or a 'thing which ought to be done' which might give rise to a duty under the Occupiers' Liability Act 1957. The 1984 Act was not relevant as the swimmers would not be trespassers. The USA's counsel also considered that it was open to the HSE to conclude that the proposal was consistent with section 3 of the Health and Safety at Work (HSAW) Act, and that the executive would be wrong to apply automatically the standards required at swimming pools, such as supervision by professional lifeguards, to a self-regulating club.

But Timothy Straker QC, in subsequent legal advice to the corporation, stated that section 3 of the HSAW Act still 'stands in the way of the Corporation permitting unsupervised early morning swimming'.[8] This view was successfully challenged in the case discussed below.

under the HSAW Act, and the way that the HSE interprets those duties, have been important in persuading some operators of country parks to curtail swimming in their lakes. Buckinghamshire County Council's ban on swimming in the lake at Black Park was a response to discussions with the HSE about the number of lifeguards required to meet its obligations under the HSAW Act.[5]

The HSE, in interpreting this act, makes a distinction between land which the public is invited, or even encouraged, to visit, and land where access is more restricted. The HSE inspector who advised Buckinghamshire County Council on the Black Park case explained that 'a private individual, whatever their business, inviting friends to swim in a pond or swimming pool in the garden of their home would not have duties under health and safety law; a farmer inviting the public to swim in a river or pond on his farm as part of his undertaking may have'.[6] It has even been argued, in legal advice to the Corporation of London, that section 3 of the HSAW Act could inhibit the corporation from allowing members of a self-regulating association from swimming in the Mixed Pond at Hampstead Heath, at their own risk and at times when the general public had no access to the pond (see box 'A Swim Before Work?'). The HSE would give no assurance that it would not prosecute the corporation if such swimming were allowed. However, in an application for judicial review brought by the Hampstead Heath Winter Swimming Club (HHWSC) against the Corporation of London, Mr Justice Stanley Burnton ruled that 'for the purposes of section 3 of the 1974 Act, if an adult swimmer with knowledge of the risks of swimming chooses to swim unsupervised, the risks he incurs are the result of his decision and not the permission given to him to swim' (*HHWSC v. Corporation of London*: para. 63).

When, in July 2004, the corporation was advised that it might face prosecution, there appeared to be a disjunction between the civil and the criminal law of England, and there had been no court decision restricting the operation of section 3 (1) of the HSAW Act in the field of criminal liability. Now, the determined winter swimmers have secured a clarification of the application of section 3 (1) which brings it more into line with recent rulings on the Occupiers' Liability Acts. Not only does the judgement mean that the Corporation of London could allow self-regulating swimming in the Mixed Pond without fearing prosecution by the HSE, it also appears to have wider implications for operators of country parks, and other sites where open-water swimming is allowed. Mr. Justice Stanley Burnton explained that 'it would be anomalous if Congleton Borough Council, so emphatically relieved by the House of Lords of liability in tort to Mr Tomlinson, were to be held to have infringed section 3 of the 1974 Act by failing to prevent his swimming in the lake. It would mean that the individual liberty that the House of Lords thought it was upholding was illusory: the criminal law would take away what the House of Lords thought it was establishing. And so I think it right to derive from the judgements in *Tomlinson* an approach to the interpretation and application of the 1974 Act in the present factual context' (*HHWSC v. Corporation of London*: para. 47).

It is clear, therefore, that safety organisations have been overzealous in seeking to restrict swimming in inland waters. Their advice to site operators not only reflects, in some cases, an erroneous interpretation of the law, but also a view that the risks of swimming in lakes and rivers are unacceptably high. The next two chapters consider how far this perception is justified.

7

THE COST OF A QUICK DIP – THE DANGER OF DROWNING

We don't want to be killjoys but this is an important message. The cost of a quick dip could be a high price to pay – don't swim in rivers, lakes or canals. Be safe and have fun by using your local swimming pool or designated swimming areas.

Irven Forbes, Environment Agency 2005

It is a fallacy to say that because drowning is a serious matter there is therefore a serious risk of drowning.

Lord Hobhouse of Woodborough (*Tomlinson v. Congleton Borough Council* 2003: para. 79)

The message from Irven Forbes was for many years the Environment Agency's regular party line, repeated each summer until about two years ago. It gave the impression that only foolhardy youths enjoy our inland waters, and that venturing into them was a uniquely dangerous thing to do. The agency no longer issues such warnings, but they still come from the Fire Services whenever they rescue someone who has fallen into the water. Here we examine the accident statistics and seek to compare the risk of swimming with other water-based activities. Do they justify the Fire Service warnings? Do they justify site managers – local authorities, water companies, and private operators – taking a more restrictive approach to bathing in lakes and rivers than to other water-based activities?

(Who drowns and what were they doing?)

More than 400 people in the UK drown accidentally each year. It is often assumed that these deaths are the result of swimming whereas, in fact, only a small proportion of people drown through getting into difficulties while swimming. In some cases we do not know what these unfortunate people were doing immediately before their deaths, but it is clear that the majority of them were engaged in other activities and, we must assume, did not intend to go into the water at all. More recent statistics indicate that, in 2009, nearly 80 per cent of people who drowned were doing things that do not normally involve getting into the water, and less than half were water-related activities (National Water Safety Forum 2011). RoSPA is now working with other organisations at the National Water Safety Forum to improve the basis on which these statistics are collected and analysed, and the data for 2009 are not directly comparable with the earlier figures quoted in tables 7.1 and 7.2 below.[1] But the pattern remains the same.

Table 7.1: Activities associated with accidental drownings in the UK

	1986		1994		2001	
	No.	%	No.	%	No.	%
Drownings with identified cause associated with						
boating	59	25	31	12	22	8
angling	44	18	39	16	16	6
fell in water	39	16	93	37	59	22
in vehicles	18	8	26	10	25	9
swimming	51	21	42	17	33	12
sub-aqua	13	5	n/a	0	18	7
canoeing	7	3	13	5	5	2
attempting rescue	7	3	5	2	n/a	0
alcohol	n/a	0	n/a	0	94	35
Total with identified cause						
	238	100	249	100	272	100
Other drownings	325		199		149	
All drownings	563		448		421	

Note: The categories listed by RoSPA vary from year to year. In some years figures were given for playing, walking, cycling and skating, which in this table are included in the 'fell-in' category, and paddling, which is added to 'swimming'.

Source: RoSPA 1987, 1995 and n.d.

The proportion of swimming-related drownings varies slightly from year to year reflecting, among other things, summer temperatures, but tends to be between 15 and 20 per cent of the total number of drownings. The summer of 1995 was a particularly hot one and saw swimming-related drownings rise to just over 20 per cent, whereas in 2001, when visitors to the countryside were severely restricted by the foot-and-mouth epidemic, fewer people drowned and the swimming-related drownings dropped to under 13 per cent of all accidental drownings.

Yet health and safety advisors have given us the impression that drowning is invariably a result of swimming. The HSE, in the foreword to the 1999 edition of its manual on the safety of swimming pools, stated that 10-12 people drown in pools every year and that 'swimming pools are far safer places to swim than open water, which claimed about 420 deaths in 1998' (HSE/Sport England 1999).[2] It failed to point out that most of the deaths in open water were not a result of swimming. Such statements help to mislead even the well-informed public – from judges to journalists. Lord Hoffman, when considering the Appeal Court's award of damages to the young man who injured himself diving into a lake at Brereton Country Park, commented that 450 people in the UK die from swimming each year, an error that was repeated in the *Times* report on the case.[3] An article by a journalist in the *Financial Times*, explaining why he decided to give up learning to swim, concluded with the comment that as non-swimmers do not swim they have little opportunity to drown (Sanghera 2004: 3). Unfortunately, this is not so.

The typical victim of drowning appears to be a young man who has been drinking too much and acting recklessly, but not necessarily swimming. Most people who drown are men between the ages of 15 and 29; relatively few are children under 15. Alcohol is an important factor, though just how important is far from clear. One study suggested that up to 80 per cent of deaths by drowning involve men where 'adventurousness, bravado, alcohol-induced foolishness and misjudgements' are contributory factors (Baylis *et al.* 1995). An earlier analysis by the Royal Life Saving Society indicated that, where known, alcohol contributed to 26 per cent of all drownings, but to 47 per cent of those in the 20-30 age group (RLSS 1983). Studies in other countries have also found a strong association between alcohol consumption and drowning. A study in Denmark, for example, found that between one-third and one-half of adult drownings were related to alcohol, again usually drunken men falling into the water (Steensberg 1998: 755-762). Alcohol is also associated with non-fatal accidents in water. Studies in the USA, for example, found spinal-cord injuries, a particular danger of diving into water, were related to the consumption of alcohol (Branche *et al.*1991 and Gabrielson *et al.* 2001).

The statistics for 2001 indicated alcohol was primarily responsible for more than a third of drownings (RoSPA n.d.). This category was not separated out in previous years, and it is not clear how to interpret it. Alcohol may have been a contributory factor in the deaths of people taking part in the other activities – whether boating, fishing, swimming or just falling into the water. It is certainly an important contributor to deaths by drowning.

Relatively few of the accidental drownings occur to children and those that do, it would appear from RoSPA's statistics, are not usually related to swimming. In 2001, 40 young people under the age of 15 are recorded as drowning accidentally, a similar figure to the previous year. The majority of these deaths resulted from children playing or walking near water; some met their deaths in home baths or garden ponds and others when the car in which they were travelling fell into the water. Only four were recorded as being associated with swimming and these accidents took place in swimming pools (RoSPA n.d.).

Where do people drown?

Although the total number of drownings appears to have been declining steadily – perhaps more markedly than the RoSPA figures suggest since the basis upon which they were compiled has changed twice since the 1980s – the pattern of drownings, in terms of where people drown, has remained fairly constant.[4] The data on location, unlike the information on the activities associated with drowning, have been more complete and presented more consistently. They show that, over the years, the largest proportion of accidental drownings have taken place in rivers and streams, with the coastal waters claiming the second largest number lives (see table 7.2). But, again, we must remember that not all these accidents were a result of swimming in these waters.

Table 7.2: Location of accidental drownings in UK

Location of drownings	1986		1994		2001	
	No	%	No.	%	No.	%
Coastal	142	25	99	22	74	18
Docks and harbours	28	5	27	6	14	3
Rivers, streams etc	200	36	167	37	171	41
Lakes and reservoirs	68	12	76	17	52	12
Canals	52	9	26	6	53	13
Home baths	32	6	28	6	31	7
Swimming pools	30	5	12	3	9	2
Garden ponds	7	1	9	2	10	2
Other	4	1	4	1	7	2
Total	563	100	448	100	421	100

Source: RoSPA 1987, 1995 and n.d.

The risks of open waters

Open waters present many dangers – but not just to swimmers. Heavy seas can wreck boats and sweep bystanders off promontories, winds can blow inflatables out to sea, just as rip currents can carry swimmers out to sea. Some rivers have dangerous currents and shallow mountain streams can become raging torrents soon after heavy rainfall. Rivers in upland areas tend to be cold even in summer. Shallow lakes, even in the mountains, can become relatively warm in summer, but deep lakes, even in lowland areas, remain cold all the year round. Both rivers and lakes may have weeds that can entangle a person's legs or underwater obstructions which, obscured by turbid water, make it dangerous to fall in as well as to jump or dive in.

But the number of people who drown in open waters – rivers, lakes and the sea – while swimming in them is actually quite small. We saw from table 7.1 that, over the years, only about one-sixth of the accidental deaths from drowning in the UK have been associated with swimming. The published figures for earlier years, before 2001, did not distinguish between those that occur in swimming pools, the sea or inland waters. Unpublished figures by RoSPA for the ten years from 1992 to 2001, indicated there were about 15 drownings a year in swimming pools: five in public pools, five in private pools such as those in hotels and gyms and five in home-based pools. Over that period 31 deaths a year were associated with swimming in open waters: about six people a year in the sea and about 25 while swimming in inland waters.[5] The figures for 2009, though compiled from more comprehensive sources and presented in a different way, show remarkably similar pattern – of the 49 drowning associated with swimming that year, 5 were in swimming pools, and 26 in inland waters (National Water Safety Forum 2011).

It is clear therefore that the absolute number of people who drown from swimming in open waters (inland and coastal) is small: about 30 a year in the UK. In order to estimate what sort of risk this represents, however, we would need to know not only how many people die from swimming in open waters but also how many people swim there. But this is something we know even less about. We can get some idea of how many people swim out-of-doors in Great Britain from the occasional surveys of leisure activities carried out as part of the General Household Survey. In 2002 (the latest date for which this information is available) the survey included an estimate of the proportion of people who swam, indoors and out-of-doors, as well as those who fished, or sailed, or went canoeing or windsurfing (Office of National Statistics 2004). An extract from these data is given in table 7.3. Unfortunately the information on outdoor swimming did not distinguish between outdoor pools, inland waters and the sea. It also related to adults of 16 years or over, which is a serious limitation since we know from various sources that many children under 16 are enthusiastic swimmers.[6] Also, the data from the General Household Survey relate to Great Britain, whereas RoSPA's data on drowning relates to the United Kingdom.

Table 7.3: Percentage of population taking part in the most popular water sports (GB, 16+ age group, 2002)

Participation

| | Swimming | | Fishing | Sailing | Canoe | Windsurfing/ |
	Indoor	Outdoor				Board sailing
In previous 12 months	30	13	6	2	2	1
4 or more times in previous 4 weeks	5	2	1	0	0	0

Source: Office of National Statistics 2004. Extract from Table 1

The General Household Survey information does, however, enable us to make a rough comparison between the risks of swimming in indoor pools and in all outdoor swimming places. RoSPA unpublished information, quoted above, distinguished between public pools, private pools (in hotels or health centres) and home pools – not between indoor and outdoor pools. But if we assume that most public and private pools are indoors and that most home pools are out-of-doors, it would appear that indoor pools account for something like one-fifth of swimming deaths but over half the number of swimmers. This is consistent with RoSPA's message that public and private swimming pools are the safest places to swim. The HSE estimates that swimming pools receive about 350 million visits a year, which result in only ten deaths (HSE/Sport England 2003: v).

It is hardly surprising to find that outdoor swimming, which includes swimming in open waters as well as outdoor pools some of which will be unsupervised private pools, is more hazardous than swimming in indoor pools. But, the question we need to answer is – just how risky is swimming in open waters – particularly rivers and lakes? And, how do the risks compare with other water-based activities, such as angling, canoeing and sub-aqua, activities that are looked upon more favourably by countryside policy makers and managers of open waters?

In attempting to answer this question we need to look at the numbers of people taking part in these activities, how often they do so and, ideally, how long they spend. The General Household Survey found that twice as many people swim out-of-doors and did so twice as often. More recently a series of studies, the Watersports and Leisure Participation Surveys, have given us much more data on numerous water-based activities including information on outdoor swimming, The survey for 2009 gives us an indication of the proportion of outdoor swimming that takes place in the sea, as distinct from inland swimming, finding that slightly more people swim at the coast than inland. It also gives us information on the number of times people take part in various water-based activities in a year but, unfortunately, not how much time they spend doing so. These data also, from our point of view, have two other serious limitations. As with the General Household Survey data, the information on outdoor swimming does not distinguish between people using outdoor swimming pools and open waters. Also, as with the General Household Survey, the data for outdoor swimming exclude children under 16 and therefore seriously underestimate the number of people who swim and, almost certainly, how often they do so.

Nevertheless, with these provisos, we can attempt to throw some light on the question of risks of wild swimming in relation to other water-based activities. Table 7.4 summarises these findings. Most surprisingly, the figures seem to suggest that the risks of outdoor swimming generally may not be so very different from angling. However, the analysis does not take into account the fact that anglers spend much longer fishing than swimmers spend in the water. It also suggests that canoeing may be a far safer activity than swimming and angling, and that sub-aqua would appear to be far more risky. The numbers of people taking part in sub-aqua are so small, however, that these figures need to be treated with more caution. Nevertheless, the analysis does call into question the policy of managers who ban swimming in their lakes or reservoirs for safety reasons, but allow sub-aqua which, though a club-based sport with safety rules and risk assessment guidelines, appears to be much more dangerous.

The risks of swimming in lakes and rivers

The above analysis does not throw much light on the risks of swimming in lakes and rivers as distinct from open waters generally. We know that most accidental drownings occur in rivers and it is often assumed, therefore, that rivers are the most risky places to swim. But we need to remember that there are many more opportunities for people to jump into, or fall into, a river than into a lake, canal or the sea. RoSPA has suggested that unsupervised swimming in inland waters is common and the Environment Agency's erstwhile warnings gave the impression that hoards of reckless youths would jump into unsuitable stretches of water on a hot day. RoSPA also acknowledged that the relatively high numbers of inland, compared to coastal, drownings could be explained in part by the fact that more people live near a river than by the sea (RoSPA 1999). There are also many more stretches of river accessible to swimmers, walkers and others, than lakes or canals. In England, in particular, we have few lakes outside the upland areas that are accessible on foot, and even fewer in which we are allowed to swim, and swimming in most canals has been forbidden. One indication that many more people swim in rivers than in lakes and canals comes from Rob Fryer's guide to wild swimming, where he lists well over 300 river swimming spots in England and Wales, but only 25 lakes and two canals (Fryer 2009). It is not surprising, therefore, that more people drown in rivers. Though we can't quantify it, the risk of swimming in rivers is likely to be lower than the crude figures imply.

Table 7.4: Selected water sports in UK – a rough indication of relative risk

Outdoor watersports	Number taking part (over 16)	Total deaths	Ratio of drownings to participants	No of events	Ratio of deaths to events
Canoeing	1,262,478	4	1 in 315,620	8,395,669	1 in 2,098,917
All outdoor swimming	4,998,774	44	1 in 113,609	24,773,994	1 in 563,045
Sea swimming	2,749,356	17	1 in 161,725	n/a	
Inland swimming	2,249,448	26	1 in 86,517	n/a	
Angling/fishing	1,330,044	27	1 in 49,261	13,978,235	1 in 517,712
Sub-aqua	444,868	17	1 in 22,243	1,947,240	1 in 114,544

Notes. Data on activities comes from the Watersports and Leisure Participation Report 2009 (tables 1, 43, and 44). These data do not include children under 16, and therefore underestimate the number of swimmers, and the frequency of swimming. Data on drowning relates to 2009, from National Water Safety Forum (2011), except for canoeing where data relates to 2005.

Public policy and the risk of drowning

Public policy has frowned upon swimming in inland waters, and most local authorities and private operators are unwilling to allow informal swimming in the waters they control, while angling and many other water sports are welcomed. Sub-aqua is allowed in some local authority lakes and the water company reservoirs where swimming is banned. Fishing is actively encouraged in many inland waters, unsupervised swimming in the sea is accepted as normal, but swimming in rivers is regarded as uniquely dangerous and to be discouraged. The data gatherers, mean-while, are not interested in collecting statistics about swimming in inland waters The Watersports and Leisure Participation Surveys, commissioned by the British Marine Federation, the Maritime and Coastguard Agency, the Royal National Lifeboat Institution and the Royal Yachting Association, and sponsored by Yachting and Boating World, have a strong bias towards boats and boating, and activities associated with the leisure industry. Informal swimming in our lakes and rivers offers little scope for commercial entrepreneurs. So, without more information, our conclusions about the relative risks must remain tentative. One thing is clear: we do not have adequate information on the risks of drowning to justify the widespread prejudice against swimming in inland waters.

We can, however, be confident that drinking alcohol when doing anything in, on or near water poses a serious risk. Waterside regeneration projects often involve waterside pubs with beer gardens overlooking rivers, canals or disused dock basins. British Waterways, which banned swimming in all its waterways, vigorously pursued a policy of developing waterside pubs on its land in its 'Waterside Pub Partnership' scheme (British Waterways 2004a) presumably unconcerned about the linkage between drinking and drowning. But no one would suggest that developing riverside pubs should be discouraged, nor that people should be forbidden a few pints of beer in their gardens, or a glass or two of white wine while punting along the river.

Another irony of the anti-swimming policies is that, by introducing and rigor-ously enforcing 'no swimming' policies in relatively safe places, site managers may divert swimmers to less safe places. This is what happened when people were suddenly prevented from swimming from the gently shelving beach in Hatchmere Lake, prompting young boys to swim instead in a more dangerous lake nearby. And this is what campaigners feared would happen when North Cornwall District Council was considering closing the popular sea pool at Bude, after an HSE inspector advised that it was dangerous on account of its uneven bottom, unclear water, and the lack of arrangements for keeping the public out of the pool when it was officially closed.[7] According to the council the sea pool had been in use for 70 years without any serious accidents. Had it not been kept open, with the help of determined volunteers, swimmers would have been tempted into the sea nearby where strong waves and rip currents often make bathing very dangerous for inex-perienced swimmers. Rather than banning unsupervised swimming in lakes and rivers, on the basis of inadequate statistics, the authorities should be considering how to enable swimmers to find relatively safe places in which to enjoy our inland waters, and accepting that there will be risks – just as they accept that there are risks involved in other water sports and waterside activities.

Although it is drowning that appears to be the main concern among site operators, swimming in inland waters is also often discouraged for health reasons. We look at the health dangers in the next chapter.

8

THE COST OF A QUICK DIP – THE HEALTH HAZARDS

Man is a territorial animal, well adapted to living in air and for whom, generally, water is a hostile environment.

Rodney Cartright *Recreational waters: a health risk?* 1992: 91

Weil's disease is the secret weapon of whatever dark forces are opposed to wild swimming.

Roger Deakin *Waterlog* 2000: 113

Weil's disease is the bogey man that stalks our inland waters. Although the Environment Agency and RoSPA no longer use him to scare us off, local authorities and water companies still appear to believe that, if we dip our toes into a river or lake, there is a high risk of contracting this deadly disease. Here we examine the risks of contracting disease from swimming in untreated freshwaters.

Water-borne diseases

However much some of us feel at home in a lake or the sea, we are nevertheless essentially terrestrial animals for whom water is a hostile environment. On entering the water we expose our bodies to potential health problems. Water can contain a variety of pathogens (algal, viral, parasitic or bacterial) resulting from both natural processes and human activities. Human, animal and industrial wastes are still discharged into some waterways, agricultural pollutants leak into rivers at many points, and birds and animals are a major source of pollution. Bathers themselves also cause pollution and, as water can spread some infections from bather to bather, crowded swimming places, even sometimes chlorinated pools, are not without some risk to health.

Not all diseases that affect humans can be transmitted by water. It was a polio scare that prompted the ban on swimming in Coate Water (see box on page 73) but it is now understood that polio is not caught in this way (PWTAG 1999: 87). Fortunately, too, for open-water swimmers, water is a hostile environment for some micro-organisms, such as salmonellae, faecal coliforms or faecal streptococci, which can cause illness in humans. These organisms perish when there are insufficient nutrients or if they are exposed to ultraviolet light. They are also sensitive to other variables, such as temperature, surviving longer in cold water. Less is known about the persistence of such organisms in fresh water than in salt water, but fresh waters appear to show greater variation in the concentration of potentially harmful micro-organisms than coastal waters (Godfree 1993).

Less is known, too, about the health dangers of swimming in lakes and rivers than in the sea. Studies of the effects of water-borne pathogens upon swimmers have focused largely on sea water and swimming pools. Information about the health effects of swimming in fresh water is limited and based mainly on small-scale studies of people engaged in other water sports such as canoeing. However, the dangers facing swimmers are similar to those facing white-water canoeists, as the water intake is likely to be similar (Pruss 1998).

What information is available, however, suggests that the health problems arising from swimming in inland waters, as in coastal waters, are generally relatively minor complaints. They are likely to be caused by swallowing water which, in most cases, leads to a mild gastrointestinal illness (Packman 1993: 225). There is also some evidence of a small increased risk of contracting an ear, nose or throat infection if we immerse ourselves in contaminated water. Whereas some earlier studies in this country suggested that the risk of catching an infection from swimming in untreated waters was negligible, even in faecally polluted waters, a more recent evaluation of 22 studies was somewhat less reassuring, finding gastrointestinal symptoms the most common problem from exposure to both fresh and marine waters (Pruss 1998). Another study of triathletes bathing in fresh water found that, even in waters that conformed to the mandatory bathing water standard, they exposed themselves to an increased risk of contracting gastroenteritis, although bathing in water that met the higher guideline standard was not associated with any significant risk. The authors of this study acknowledged, however, that the risk for triathletes might be greater than it would be for ordinary swimmers, owing to the intensity of their exposure and a temporary decrease in their immune response (Van Asperen et al 1998). Even so, the infections these athletes experienced were relatively minor ones.

These studies do not include information about more serious infections such as hepatitis, typhoid and leptospirosis (which includes Weil's disease). Water may also be contaminated by toxins and chemicals, but the effects of these upon human health are poorly understood (Stanwell-Smith 1993: 27). We do know, however, that the chances of becoming seriously ill from the two health hazards that are often associated with fresh waters – Weil's disease and blue-green algae – are small.

Weil's disease

It is Weil's disease that seems to be most feared by the public. This is hardly surprising since for many years the Environment Agency issued grave warnings, and British Waterways, water companies and local councils invoked Weil's as a major reason for banning swimming in the waters they control.

Weil's disease is one of a group of leptospiral infections, bacterial diseases, which include Swineherd's disease (*L. pomona*), Stuttgart disease (*L. canicola*) as well as the more serious Weil's disease (*L. icterohaemorrhagiae*). Leptospirosis is caught by humans when open wounds come into contact with infected urine (usually from rodents, dogs, cattle or sheep) or urine-infected soil or water. It can survive for several months in fresh water or moist alkaline soil, but does not survive for more than a few hours in salt water. Weil's disease, the most serious form of leptospirosis, can be fatal. Fortunately, however, it is very rare and is seldom contracted by swimmers or others engaged in water sports.

Leptospiral infections are among the notifiable diseases that doctors in England and Wales must report to local authorities. Thus, although some mild cases may not be reported, we must assume that at least the most serious cases will have been. In the ten years from 1980 to 1989 there were 533 reported cases of leptospiral infections in the UK, mainly from *leptospira hardjo*, a serotype associated mainly with cattle. Over the same period there was a total of 25 deaths – on average less than 3 a year (Fewtrell and Jones 1992). Since then the incidence of infections in England and Wales seems to have increased slightly, or perhaps the reporting has been more complete, with an average of 40 cases being reported each year. Deaths from leptospirosis, however, have become even rarer, with only three cases between 1996 and 2009.[1]

Table 8.1: Reported cases of leptospiral infections (England and Wales, 1990-1995)

Year	Quarter ending				
	March	June	Sept	Dec	Total for year
1990	4	1	7	8	20
1991	7	3	4	7	21
1992	4	2	10	12	28
1993	6	5	4	3	18
1994	8	6	7	4	25
1995	6	6	7	4	23
Quarterly totals	35	23	39	38	135

Source: OPCS Monitor 1992 to 1996

Weil's disease, therefore, is seldom fatal and swimmers are not the most likely people to catch the disease. Leptospirosis is much more prevalent in tropical and sub-tropical countries and, in recent years, increasingly infections are being brought back by travellers from warmer climates. In this country it is an occupational hazard for farmers, particularly those working with animals and in waste management. In 2009, of the cases recorded in England and Wales, 14 were contracted abroad, 11 were related to farming and other high risk occupations,

NO SWIMMING NOW IN THE NEW SEA

In Richard Jefferies' classic novel *Bevis* two boys, Bevis and his friend Mark, swim and fish in the New Sea, build a boat to explore its waters, and camp on the island. The nineteenth-century naturalist and writer was recalling his own unfettered boyhood when he lived beside Coate Water. This 56-acre lake, on the south-west edge of Swindon, was constructed in the 1820s as a headwater tank for the Wiltshire and Berkshire Canal. When the fortunes of the canal company waned with the coming of the railway, the reservoir became redundant. In 1914 the public-spirited Swindon Corporation bought the lake and 80 acres of adjacent land for the people of Swindon. The introduction to the 1930 edition of *Bevis* praises the new guardians of the lake and its surroundings for keeping them 'as lovely and free – or nearly so – as the days when Bevis built his boat' (Jefferies 1930: xvi-xvii).

For many years the lake continued to be enjoyed by swimmers. A splendid art deco diving board was built in 1936 and the lake hosted diving competitions and water polo matches. But swimming was stopped in 1958 after a polio scare. Now you can fish or sail, watch birds from a hide, play in the purpose-built play areas, picnic and barbecue, try pitch-and-putt or miniature golf, hire a bicycle or join an orienteering session. But you cannot swim. The main reason now is the fear of litigation, were an accident to occur, and the cost of ensuring safety in a busy park. Another reason is the recurrence of blue-green algae each August. It is a problem, say park managers, that is difficult to solve in a large lake with nutrient-rich water where barley-straw rafts would interfere with the other users of the lake.[5] The Canada geese don't help. The water near the deserted diving board is so murky with their droppings and half-eaten slices of bread that few would want to swim there now, although in other parts of the lakes it is more inviting.

Coate Water is a Site of Special Scientific Interest, providing nesting sites for waterfowl, reed bunting and warblers, and a habitat for dragon flies and damsel flies. Jefferies would be pleased they are protected but he would be sad that we can no longer swim in his New Sea.

seven were people who had taken part in water sports (canoeing, fishing, sailing, windsurfing, swimming), six were acquired at home (from rats and mice or cleaning ditches or drains), and two from accidental immersion.[2] Were leptospirosis a high risk for swimmers one would expect the rate of infection to rise in the summer but, as table 8.1 shows, the incidence, at least in England and Wales, is spread fairly evenly throughout the year. Even in the glorious summer of 2003 there was no peak in such infections in the summer months.[3] The risk is generally thought to be greater in urban waters. Yet at Henleaze Swimming Club's lake in Bristol, which on a busy day gets 500 to 600 swimmers, there has never been a proven case of Weil's disease in the club's well-recorded 90 years of swimming history.[4]

The disused diving platform at Coate Water

Blue-green algae

Managers of country parks and water companies often mention the seasonal occurrence of blue-green algae as one of the reasons why they do not allow swimming in their lakes or reservoirs. Until recently the Environment Agency would also cite blue-green algae in its annual warning against swimming in inland waters. It is one of the reasons given for the continuing ban on swimming in Coate Water, another lake with a long swimming history (see box on previous page 'No Swimming Now in the New Sea').

Blue-green algae, toxic blooms of cyanobacteria, are most likely to occur during hot summers in lakes in lowland England where the waters are enriched with nitrogen and phosphorus. RoSPA warns us that contact with blue-green algae can cause dermatitis, asthma, eye irritation and rashes (RoSPA 1999). However, in a comprehensive survey of pathogenic organisms in temperate water, Fewtrell and colleagues reported that, although there have been reports of animal deaths, there have been no known human deaths anywhere in the world caused by cyanobacterial toxins (Fewtrell *et al* 1994). Even RoSPA admits that the risks posed by blue-green algae are low (RoSPA 1999).

It is a problem that we may expect to get worse with global warming but, unlike other pathogens that may be lurking in the water, the toxic blooms can often be seen, at least when they form a scum which tends to drift and collect at the edges of a lake, and thus they are more easily avoided by people considering whether to swim (NRA 1990: para. 7.13). If no scum is visible, however, there may still be large numbers of algae below the surface of the water to irritate the skin of swimmers. This is likely to be more of a problem for people using wet suits than for casual swimmers, as the algal material may get trapped inside a wet suit and remain in contact with the skin for some time (NRA 1990: para 7.14). Managers of some small lakes have found floating bales of barley straw helpful in controlling this problem, but it does not work well for large or very enriched (eutrophic) lakes. In a small lake it may be possible simply to rake the filaments out of the water, perhaps suspending swimmer for a day – but not for the season.

Health concerns about swimming pools

Since we are warned against swimming in lakes and rivers and encouraged to swim instead in swimming pools, it is worth remembering that even swimming pools are not without some risks to health. Such risks may arise, particularly in a badly managed pool, as swimming pools tend to be more crowded than natural swimming places and it is the bathers themselves who are the major source of pollution. Thomas van Leeuvan, in his history of swimming pools, claims that 'With the first plunge the average bather introduces 600 million microbes, while a class of children pollutes a basically clean pool in a couple of seconds' (Van Leeuvan 1998: 258). This could make a chlorinated pool less healthy than some untreated, but less crowded, waters. A study of several bathing sites in the United States – on Lake Michigan, the Ohio River, a chlorinated freshwater pool and the tidal water of Long Island Sound – found the highest incidence of illness at the chlorinated pool (Kay and Wyer 1992).

Both here and in the USA reports of infections attributable to swimming pools are better documented than those traceable to swimming in natural waters, since more people swim in pools and the systems for monitoring them are more likely to be in place. The illnesses caused by infections caught in swimming pools are not usually life threatening. One of the most problematic is *cryptosporidium*, which causes diarrhoea, as it is relatively resistant to chlorine-based disinfectants; but it can be controlled by coagulation and filtration.[6] Potentially more serious is *legionella pneumophila*, a respiratory infection which, like *pseudomonas aeruginosa* causing folliculitis and ear infections, is killed by chlorine; but this tends to be associated with spa baths rather than swimming pools (PWTAG 1999). Even hydrotherapy pools can expose the patients using them to infection (Stanwell-Smith 1993).

In addition to the possibility of picking up infections from faecal pollution, often caused by other bathers, there is now increasing concern about the exposure to the chemicals, particularly chlorine, which are used to disinfect the pools. Chlorine compounds, used to kill pathogens, release hypochlorous acid which reacts with organic matter brought in by swimmers (such as urine and fragments of skin) to generate potentially harmful by-products including trihalomethanes (THMs), trihaloacetic acids and chloramines. THMs can be absorbed from the water though the skin or inhaled from the air above the water's surface. A recent study of eight indoor pools in London found a relatively high concentration of trihalomethanes. The authors note that previous studies have shown a high take-up of THMs by swimmers and that there is some evidence, though this is not conclusive, of an association between exposure to THMs and reproductive problems. They suggest it may pose a health risk, particularly for pregnant women, and therefore needs further study (Chu and Nieuwenhuijsen 2002).

It has been know for some time that another by-product of chlorination, nitrogen trichloride, is a powerful irritant which can cause acute lung injury in accidental exposure to chlorine-based disinfectants and cleaning materials. But it is only recently that researchers have begun to study the possible effects on swimmers. A recent epidemiological study, the first of its kind, found evidence of damage to the lungs of young children who swim regularly in chlorinated pools (Bernard *et al.* 2003). Other researchers have questioned the validity of the statistical analyses employed, suggesting that the association between asthma and swimming pools may have been overstated. This criticism was rejected by the authors who reported that their subsequent study, which explored more specifically the links between asthma, lung inflammation, atopy and cumulated exposure to pool chlorine, indicated that the association was far from being overstated (Armstrong and Strachan 2004).

In the United States concerns about the dangers of swimming-pool chemicals has reached such a degree that, according to Van Leeuvan, their toxicity has driven swimmers to wear frogman's suits and protective masks. This follows reports of a study which found erosion of swimmers' front teeth from frequent exposure to water that was over-chlorinated and too acid.

Research into the health problems associated with swimming-pool chemicals is at an early stage and by no means conclusive. The powerful disinfectants are essential for crowded swimming pools and the benefits of chlorination almost certainly outweigh the possible hazards. There are now moves towards supplementing chlorine-based disinfectants with other treatments such as ozone and ultra-violet light which, together with better ventilation of indoor pools, helps to reduce the level of undesirable THMs in the pool area. Nevertheless, although we can be sure that supervised swimming pools are safer than open waters from the point of view of drowning, it is not clear how far they are always safer from a health point of view – especially as lakes and rivers vary considerably in their water quality.

Bathing-water quality

Any discussion of the health risks of swimming in untreated water is complicated by the fact that such waters vary in quality. There is also disagreement about the appropriate indicators to be used to test whether water is safe for bathing.

Many inland waters are now of good quality. Our rivers have been getting steadily cleaner, and by 2009 73 per cent of English rivers, and 87 per cent of those in Wales, were judged to be of good biological quality.[7] And many lakes have even better water. Research by the Water Research Centre found that, in terms of faecal coliforms, lakes and reservoirs generally have better water quality than coastal waters, which in turn are generally better than estuaries and rivers (Grantham 1993: 221-222). In some lakes, such as those on sandy heaths or flooded sand and gravel pits, the sand and gravel act as an effective cleansing filter for the water seeping into the lake. In addition, the storage of water in an enclosed basin reduces the concentration of enteric bacteria and pathogens, as the micro-organisms die with time and thus, if no further pollutants are added, the water quality improves. Studies in London, Salford and Liverpool, for example, have shown that water of exceptional biological quality can be achieved and maintained within an enclosed dock basin. Many fresh water lakes have been found to contain such low levels of microbiological contamination that they would have complied with the requirements of the Bathing Water Directive (Godfree 1993: 150).

But there has been, and continues to be, some disagreement over the indicators that were used to test bathing waters under the Bathing Water Directive especially for inland waters. Counts of faecal coliforms, the indicator formerly used in relation to the mandatory standard, was not considered to be the best measure of risk. In a comparative study of several bathing sites in the United States the chlorinated pool which was associated with the highest morbidity had the lowest coliform count. It was suggested that the presence of faecal streptococci (formerly used in testing for the higher guideline standard) was a better indicator of risk of gastrointestinal problems (Philipp et al 1985). Other studies have indicated that enteroviruses (such as those that cause hepatitis A) may be better indicators of serious health risks than bacteria, and that different standards may be needed for different activities (Fewtrell and Jones 1992).

In drawing up proposals for the revised EC Bathing Water Directive the Commission acknowledged that more research was needed into viral indicators. On the basis of its review of recent research, however, the commission concluded that bathing-water quality would be tested in future on two key microbiological parameters, intestinal enterococci and escherischia coli, both bacterial indicators, instead of the previous nineteen, complemented by visual inspections for algal bloom and oil and, for fresh waters, measurement of their acidity (Commission of the European Communities 2002).

Public policy and the health risks

We cannot begin to quantify the risks to health from swimming in untreated inland waters, but the evidence suggests that they are low. It would appear that public authorities exaggerate the health hazards even more than they exaggerate the risks of drowning. They ignore the fact that these health risks are also faced by people engaged in other water-contact activities, such as sub-aqua, water-skiing, wind-surfing and white-water canoeing. Triathlons and sub-aqua clubs may be allowed to use waters where casual swimming is banned, although triathletes are more likely to succumb to infection than casual bathers and people using wet suits may be more at risk from blue-green algae.

It seems that the health risks are often an excuse, rather than a genuine reason, for banning swimming. Certainly, the threat of Weil's disease and blue-green algae has been be used deliberately to scare people who might otherwise be tempted to swim. As we saw in the case of Brereton Country Park (featured in the box on page 57) it does not always work. We do not know how many people would like to swim but are deterred by this frequently repeated propaganda. In the next chapter we explore how many people wish to swim in lakes and rivers but, for a variety of reasons, do not do so.

9

WHO WANTS TO SWIM?

We had no toys, no books and we didn't play cricket or football. But all the boys and young men swam naked in the river in summer time. It was our biggest happiness.

Leonard Thompson, farm worker in *Akenfield* (Blythe 1969: 34)

Although there are many of us, we are still a minority, or at least we are perceived as a minority. Certainly we are seen as out of the ordinary, unconventional, eccentric. A category that is easy to, and therefore should be, controlled, restricted, and finally better still, stamped out.

Rob Fryer *Directory of Cool Places* (2003: 10)

The men and boys in the Suffolk village of Akenfield, who so enjoyed swimming in the river at the beginning of the twentieth century, were living at a time when there were far fewer purpose-built swimming pools than there are now. You may well ask: who wants to swim in lakes and rivers today? Is it an outmoded form of pleasure? Is it just a few odd-balls who want to immerse themselves in unchlorinated, sometimes muddy and often cold water? Or are there other people who would like to swim in rivers and lakes but who, for a variety of reasons, are inhibited from doing so? In this chapter we seek clues to the hidden demand for wild swimming.

How many people swim?

The public authorities, when allocating resources for recreational facilities or encouraging others to provide them, estimate demand from current patterns of activity and how they have been changing. But, as we saw in chapter 7 when trying to estimate the risk of drowning, we simply do not know how many people swim in rivers and lakes today, for open-water swimming has been ignored not just by policy makers but also by those conducting surveys of countryside activities.

Despite the popularity of swimming generally, after the 1970s, studies of recreational activities by the former Countryside Commission, tourism authorities and academics ignored open-water swimming. The 1998 Day Visits Survey, for example, seeking information on the habits and characteristics of people going out for the day, limited its question about swimming to swimming pools and leisure centres

(Countryside Agency 1999). Academic studies of countryside recreation trends and policies, also ignored wild swimming (Glyptis 1991, Harrison 1991, Curry 1994). Even where, occasionally, swimming might appear in a table of participation, the text would go on to discuss fishing or canoeing rather than swimming. Open-water swimming, like women of a certain age, became invisible.

More recent surveys, as we saw in chapter 7, have given us data on outdoor swimming, and they all point to its immense popularity. The General Household Survey in 2002 included questions about leisure and sport, finding that 12.5 per cent of adults in Britain had swum out of doors in the previous year (ONS 2004). This was not only twice as many as those who went fishing, but also slightly more than those who played golf or outdoor soccer or went running (see table 9.1). The more recent surveys that focused specifically on water-based sports and leisure activities, which we used to elucidate the relative risks of different water sports, found four times as many people swam out of doors than went fishing (British Marine Federation et al. 2009).[1] But all these studies excluded children under 16 and none of them distinguished between the use of outdoor swimming pools and open waters.

Table 9.1: Most popular outdoor activities of population (GB, 16+ age group, 2002)

Sport	Walking	Cycling	Outdoor swimming	Golf	Running/ jogging	Soccer
Percentage of population taking part in previous 12 months	45.9	19.1	12.5	12.1	9.1	7.6

Source: ONS 2004. Extract from Table 1

How many would like to swim?

What people do in their leisure time is not necessarily what they would most like to do. There do not, however, appear to be any studies that have sought to find out how many people would like to swim in lakes and rivers were they able to do so. We know little about the latent demand for open-water swimming, whether in inland or in coastal waters. A pioneering study in the field of countryside recreation in the 1960s investigated both the participation in, and the latent demand for, countryside recreation, and it did encompass outdoor swimming (British Travel Association and University of Keele 1967). It found that outdoor swimming was the most actively pursued of all outdoor recreations. 11 per cent of those questioned had swum out-of-doors during 1965. The next most frequently pursued activities were fishing and hiking, each of which were undertaken by 5 per cent of respondents. This study also asked questions about which activities people would most like to take up, and which they actually planned to take up, in the future. Despite the already high level of participation, outdoor swimming (which at that time, for most people, probably meant open-water swimming) came near the top of the list of activities that people would most like to do in future. Only sailing (on the sea and inland) and golf came higher on this wish list. Subsequent decades did indeed see an increase in people sailing, playing golf and swimming, but we do not know how far the increase in outdoor swimming, indicated in the GHS data, is accounted for by the increase in the use of outdoor swimming pools.

The GHS survey in 2002 included, for the first time, questions about which sports or physical activity people would like to take up. Swimming, again, came top of the list: 13 per cent of respondents opted for swimming and 12 per cent for keep fit or yoga; 5 per cent said they would like to play golf and the same percentage mentioned horse riding and skiing or snow-boarding. But, again, we do not know how many of these would-be swimmers would like to swim in lakes and rivers.

Given this lack of interest in open-water swimming by researchers and policy makers, it was surprising to see the Rural White Paper, published in 2000, claim that 'many people would like more freedom to swim and undertake other activities on waterways, ponds and lakes' (2000 (b): para. 11.3.10). The white paper promised to commission research into access to water for sport and recreation in order to inform future strategy. However, the subsequent study commissioned by DEFRA into the demand for, and supply of, opportunities for water-based recreation, ignored swimming (University of Brighton 2002). This omission is partly explained by the study's approach, which sought much of its information from interviews with the national organisations responsible for promoting particular water sports and from a questionnaire sent to local clubs and groups engaged in such sports. Thus open-water swimming, which is largely an informal activity and at that time did not have a national organisation to represent its interests, was neglected. The Amateur Swimming Association, the governing body for organised competitive swimming in England, does not encourage informal swimming in lakes and rivers.[2]

The University of Brighton study acknowledged that swimming takes place informally in inland waters, but did not attempt to estimate how many people swim and, though it discussed the aspirations of people engaged in minority activities such as sub-aqua, it failed to explore the aspirations of would-be swimmers. It made no recommendations about how to accommodate their interests. It did report that discussions among focus groups revealed that some people were deterred from swimming through fear of pollution, and that some would like to swim in places like the Broads were the water cleaner, but these clues were not followed up.

There has been much criticism among academics writing about countryside policy of the fact that local authorities, especially in their country parks, have planned for what they think people should do, such as walking, picnicking, bird-watching and following nature trails, rather than what they want to do, and that money has been spent on expensive visitor centres that few people use.[3] It has been

Swimmers enjoying Henleaze Lake, July 1989 (Photograph: © Derek Klemperer)

suggested that the bias towards 'quiet enjoyment' of the countryside has inhibited the growth of a full range of water sports (Harrison 1991: 153). As we saw in chapter 5, there has indeed been a bias in favour of low-impact activities – a bias that can be defended on environmental grounds – but swimming, also a low impact activity, has not been so favoured, nor have efforts been made to explore whether people want to swim.

Popular bathing places

Though we lack survey information to measure the hidden demand for open-water swimming, we do know that swimming in lakes and rivers can be very popular where the conditions are good and where swimming is clearly acceptable.

Above the weir at Farleigh Hungerford the river Frome flows deep, cool and inviting between grassy meadows. Here, in the 1930s, a swimming club was formed with the blessing of the owners of the south bank of the river and, unlike many other swimming clubs that flourished in the early twentieth century, it has continued to be popular with local swimmers (Fryer 2003). In 1992 the future of the club was threatened when the south bank was sold to a new owner, but luckily the owners of the north bank invited the club to move across the river. So the club continues to thrive, with more than 2,000 members. Visitors can become members for the day for a small fee. There are two indoor swimming pools within three miles of the club, but the continuing popularity of Farleigh indicates that wild swimming

A CITY OASIS – HENLEAZE SWIMMING CLUB

Up and down the country there must be hundreds of old quarries that provided stone to build our towns and villages or limestone to burn in lime kilns. Some have been filled in with rubbish; others have become valuable wildlife havens. Some remain as water-filled pits, perhaps fenced off and derelict or leased to an angling club. The long, deep quarry in northern Bristol is unusual for it is home to one of England's oldest open-water swimming clubs.

When quarrying for limestone ceased in 1912 and the pit was allowed to flood, it became a popular spot with swimmers until, after a drowning, the owner forbade swimming. But in 1919 a group of enthusiasts banded together to form a swimming club, enabling swimming to resume under the strict rules of the Amateur Swimming Association. The club prospered and, in 1933, was able to buy the lake and surrounding land, thus ensuring its future.

The club's members became very active, competing in championship events for swimming and diving at county, national and international level, as well as in lifesaving competitions and water polo matches. After the Second World War much of the competitive swimming transferred to a separate indoor club, and for a while the popularity of the outdoor club waned. But now it flourishes again, with a long waiting list of people anxious to join.

The bathers use one end of the long narrow lake, with grassy banks and trees, and changing facilities, showers and lavatories. The 10 metre platform of the diving tower, which was much enjoyed by intrepid divers and had been used without mishap since the 1920s, was taken out of use in 1991 on health and safety advice (see photograph opposite). At the other end the lake is bounded by high cliffs and reached by a boardwalk. Here the waters are fished by members of the Henleaze Angling Club. As the lake is open for swimming in summer only but fishing is allowed for most of the year, anglers keep an eye on the premises in the winter months. There is some concern among swimmers that fish stocks are too high, and should be reduced to improve the water quality for swimming but, generally, in this delightful urban oasis, swimmers and anglers happily coexist.

provides an experience which cannot be met by conventional swimming pools.

Swimmers at the Henleaze Swimming Club in Bristol use part of a long narrow lake, set deep within a former quarry where the high cliff walls screen out the view of surrounding houses. The club has an even longer history than Farleigh Hungerford, for swimming has taken place here since it was formed in 1919 (see box above). In 1933 the club acquired the site, thus safeguarding its future. It, too, is very popular, with a membership limited to 1,350 and several hundred would-be members on its waiting list. Members can bring guests and these account for about 2,500 further swimmers each year.

Family fun at Keynes Country Park, summer 2003.

Another popular bathing place is at Cotswold Country Park, formerly know as Keynes Country Park. where a small bathing area has been created in a former gravel pit. The lake's water, having been filtered though sand and gravel, has for years met the higher guideline standard of the Bathing Water Directive. The beach has a café, lavatories and a barbecue area, and is supervised by lifeguards. On the day that I visited the beach, a hot weekday in August, there was no doubt about its popularity – one could hardly see the water between the bathers and their inflatables, let alone try to swim. The area allocated for bathing is tiny, about 100 by 30 metres, just one small corner of a much larger lake – fine for small children but frustrating for older children and adult swimmers. If you stray beyond the barrier into the enticing lake beyond, however, lifeguards insist you come back. This inland beach, like the swimming clubs at Farleigh and Henleaze, demonstrates how well-used and well-loved good swimming places can be.

Protests when bathing is banned

The anger and disappointment displayed when a popular bathing area is closed, and the resistance to 'no swimming' signs at some traditional bathing spots, also show that some people remain passionately attached to bathing in natural waters. At Brereton Country Park, as we saw in chapter 6 and the box on page 57, attempts by the local authority to stop people bathing in the lake were resisted so resolutely that the council felt obliged to block the entrance to the site and destroy the beach. Equally, Buckinghamshire County Council's decision to prohibit bathing at Black Park

RESCUING HATCHMERE LAKE

Hatchmere Lake in Cheshire is a Site of Special Scientific Interest and also a local beauty spot where for many years people have enjoyed picnicking and birdwatching on its shores, and fishing and swimming in its gently shelving waters. Such a lake needs careful management.

When the Cheshire Wildlife Trust acquired the site in 1998, with grants from the Heritage Lottery Fund, the Countryside Agency and the local borough council, its future appeared to be in good hands. The trust appointed a local angling society to manage the site and the society proceeded to fence off the lake from its sandy beach and to plant reeds to prevent swimmers entering the water. It discouraged parking and banned swimming while, elsewhere in the lake, it built new fishing platforms and cut back reeds for the convenience of anglers. The trust claimed that these changes were designed to protect wildlife.

Swimmers were dismayed, and not only swimmers. Local ecologist, Jonathan Guest, pointed out that the trust had not carried out the investigations needed to justify such changes. It had not done a detailed survey; it had not identified the location of important species to be protected, nor considered such questions as vegetational succession or the dangers of rampant alien species being introduced by fishermen. Guest argued that planting reeds in the last sandy bay, to obstruct paddlers and swimmers, reduced the structural diversity of the shoreline and would harm one of the rare species of beetle (*gyrinus bicolor*) that inhabited the lake. He concluded that the site, bought with public money as a nature reserve, was being managed simply as a fishing pond.[4]

The swimmers and picnickers fought back, removing the fence and cutting down the reeds that blocked access to the lake. The Friends of Hatchmere Lake was formed and waged a vigorous media campaign, pointing out that a condition of the Lottery grant required the lake, and all its facilities, to remain open to the public. Eventually the parking area was restored and a swimming zone agreed. The sandy bay is no longer fenced off; picnickers, sun-bathers and swimmers can once again can enjoy the lake and its grassy slopes – perhaps the beetles can too. But from time to time the anglers try to extend their territory. It remains a precarious victory.

Country Park was met with angry protests. Regular swimmers organised protest swims and 500 people signed a petition but, so far, to no avail (see the box on page 51).

Sometimes the protestors do prevail. When the traditional swimming area was blocked and swimming banned at Hatchmere Lake in Cheshire, as we see in the box above, the decision met with such determined local opposition and media attention that it was reversed. The swimmers there were no doubt lucky to have an open-water swimming activist, Yakov Lev, to help them pursue their cause. In the early 1990s, when the new owner of the mill at Heytesbury in Wiltshire sought to divert the right of way to the millpond and stop people bathing there, he also met with protects. Again the protesters were successful although, in this case, subsequent changes to the banks destroyed the attraction of that popular bathing spot (Fryer 2003). The determined campaign by swimmers to be allowed to swim early on winter mornings, at their own risk, in the Mixed Pond on Hampstead Heath, also demonstrates the passionate concern of open-water swimmers not to lose opportunities to enjoy much-loved swimming places. In this case the protestors have not only secured a victory for themselves but also, as explained in chapter 6, they have helped to clarify the interpretation of section 3 of the Health and Safety at Work Act so that landowners will no longer need to fear prosecution by the Health and Safety Executive if they fail to prevent people from swimming on their property.

If only …

We know that some people are deterred from swimming by fears of pollution. It is likely that others are put off by the scare stories about Weil's disease, and we know that still others would love to swim if they could find suitable spots to do so. All too often we see 'no swimming' notices, but rarely are there any signs to indicate places where one is allowed to swim. At the two bathing sites owned by the National Trust on Lake Windermere, both official 'bathing waters' under the Bathing Water Directive, there is virtually nothing to alert visitors to the fact that here is a place where it is relatively safe to swim, where the water quality is good and where people are allowed to swim. These bathing places are featured in the box on page 113. The Environment Agency tests the waters at these sites but does not proclaim them as official bathing places.

In response to the negative attitude of the Health and Safety Executive, RoSPA, the Environment Agency and many local authorities towards wild swimming, as well as the difficulties in finding good places to swim, the River and Lake Swimming Association (RALSA) was set up in 2003 to give a voice to open-water swimmers. RALSA aims to:

- increase public awareness of the fact that swimming in open water is a natural, healthy and ecologically friendly sport;
- improve safety standards through information, education and vigilance and expose the consequences of the negative attitude adopted by some organisations towards swimming in rivers and lakes;
- protect the interest of swimmers whenever they come under threat and seek to remedy situations where the rights of swimmers have been or are being violated;
- restore respectability to open-water swimming;
- seek co-operation with organisations who share common interests.

The association's website enables people to share information about where they can swim and alerts them to threats to take away such opportunities.[5] Posted on its message board in the hot summer of 2003 there were many pleas for information about where people could swim near their homes. Most of these would-be swimmers were living in the Midlands and in southern counties. One contributor asked, for example, whether anyone now dares to swim in a lake on the Longleat estate, where she knows that people used to swim, but hesitates to do so herself. She added that, were she able to do so, she could swim every morning instead of driving twice a week to Farleigh Hungerford.

At Farleigh and Henleaze, Hatchmere and Hampstead Heath, where the conditions are good for swimming, the people who go there do so with the confidence that not only are the waters relatively safe and unpolluted, but also that swimming is permissible and acceptable. It is neither prohibited by the authorities, nor is it regarded as a slightly odd thing to do. The latter point is, I suspect, crucial. Everyone knows that one is allowed to swim in the sea, and everyone – not just exuberant youths but hesitant mums and wrinkly grandmothers – can do so knowing that it is regarded as a normal thing to do. Gwen Raverat gazed at the working-class boys enjoying the river Cam unable, at that time, to join them. Later, as social attitudes became more relaxed, she too could enjoy swimming in the river. But as today's rivers and lakes are generally not regarded as places to swim, one wonders how many people are once again inhibited by the feeling that it 'just isn't done'. We cannot know how many people look longingly at a clear lake or river and think ... if only.

It is clear that more people would love to be able to swim in our inland waters. We do not know how many, probably they are relatively few. But, as we glimpsed in the first chapter, for those that do, wild swimming is a deeply satisfying pleasure. Since it does not appear to be much more hazardous than some other activities that managers of inland waters allow, is it not reasonable to expect them to accept swimmers too and, in ideal places, make conditions easier and better for them?

There are also broader reasons why we should regard wild swimming as an activity to be welcomed. We explore those reasons in the next two chapters.

10

TO COOL IN THE DOG DAYS –
HEALTH AND HAPPINESS

The general effects ... [of bathing in rivers] ... are to cool in the dog days, to cleanse and moisten the skin; it cures thirst, causes sleep, produces much urine, prevents fevers, and feeds thin bodies, and, creates them an appetite, and helps their digestion.

Sir John Floyer *The History of Cold Bathing,* 1700 [1]

I never concern myself about the good or harm swimming does to me, or whether it will lengthen or shorten my life. It has enabled me to live more fully and happily. And that in itself is enough.

Jack Overhill *Swimming for Fun,* 1945

Medical opinion, over the years, has fluctuated widely in its view of water as an agent of harm or healing. In the Middle Ages water was regarded as essentially dangerous, even for washing; physicians later extolled the healing properties of mineral springs and then moved on to recommend drinking sea water and bathing in the sea. We now know that exposure to untreated waters (and sometimes treated wasters) brings a risk of contracting a water-borne infection but, as we saw in chapter 8, these risks have been exaggerated by the Environment Agency, local authorities and safety organisations. In any case, they need to be seen in the context of the benefits to our health and well-being of physical exercise. Here we look at the health benefits of swimming in open waters, as well as the more general benefits to be gained from exercise in the open air and natural surroundings.

Swimming and health

Swimming has long been recognised as one of the most beneficial forms of physical activity and one that can be undertaken by people of all ages and with a range of abilities. Swimming improves stamina and coordination, exercises more muscle groups than any other sport, encourages the heart and lungs to work more efficiently and puts little strain on the body. Rhythmic activities, such as swimming, brisk walking and dancing, are also particularly effective in inducing positive changes in mood (Department of Health 2004: 62). Swimming is important for many people with disabilities; it is one of the few active sports that they can participate in, and is particularly popular among young people with disabilities (Sport England 2001). Being a low-impact activity, however, it does not bring the benefits of weight-bearing activities, such as walking or tennis, which are important in bone formation and may protect against osteoporosis.

Water-based exercise can have an important therapeutic role in a number of conditions. A comparative study of patients with osteoarthritis found that the group attending a community-based water exercise programme experienced less pain, less functional disability, and less anxiety and depression than the control group attending the rheumatic-disease clinic. This is in line with other studies, which have found that low-impact activities, such as walking and swimming, correlate positively with a reduction in osteoarthritic pain (Cousins and Horne 1999: 109). Such studies are supported by much anecdotal evidence from practitioners of the therapeutic benefits. The Association of Swimming Therapy argues that, under controlled conditions and with medical supervision, it can play a useful role in returning the body to normal functioning after an injury or heart attack (Association of Swimming Therapy 1992). Swimming in a hydrotherapy pool has also been found to bring dramatic improvements in the behaviour of elderly patients suffering from Alzheimer's disease (Jackson 2002).

Effects of cold water on the body

Swimming or exercising in a warm hydrotherapy pool under careful supervision is, however, very different from swimming out-of-doors in lakes and rivers. Can swimming out-of-doors, in untreated wasters which are often cool, sometimes very cold, also bring health benefits?

There is no question that cold water can be injurious to health. Sudden immersion in cold water can be fatal, particularly for elderly people. Cold water impairs the ability of muscles to function effectively, even for the young and fit, thus reducing swimming performance, and this could lead to drowning. Also, prolonged exposure to cold, or even relatively warm, water can cause hypothermia – although this is more likely to be the result of accidental exposure to water than deliberate swimming.

On the other hand many hardy, all-the-year-round outdoor swimmers believe that regular immersion in cold water helps to keep them fit and healthy. The belief in the therapeutic effects of immersion in cold water has a long history. In the late sixteenth century physicians were promoting cold-water cures especially for treating melancholy, and in the late seventeenth and early eighteenth century cold water was recommended for many other complaints (Lencek and Bosker 1998: 74). Such beliefs provided the impetus for the development of sea bathing, which at first tended to be a winter activity, and underpinned the regime of cold baths and outdoor bathing in English public schools. It is tempting now to assume that the avowed health effects of all-the-year-round bathing are just a reflection of the bathers' generally healthy lifestyles and the tendency for only fit and healthy people to choose to expose themselves to the rigours of winter swimming. Recent research, however, suggests that there may be some scientific basis for the idea that regular bathing in cold water can bring some specific benefits to health.

Whereas long term exposure of humans and other animals to extreme cold leads to organ damage and death, intensive short term exposure may lead to adaptive responses that can have beneficial effects. In Germany about 3,000 people are members of winter-swimming clubs and thousands more are accustomed to winter swimming. Medical researchers there have noted that this extreme form of body hardening appears to increase people's resistance to diseases, especially to acute respiratory diseases. One such study found that regular winter swimmers experienced 40 per cent fewer infections of the upper respiratory tract than the control group. In a subsequent study Siems and colleagues sought to elucidate the biochemical mechanisms that underlie these findings. They compared blood samples from a group of winter swimmers, taken before and after swimming in ice-cold water, and from a control group of healthy people who had never participated in winter swimming or other cold-hardening procedures. The results indicated that the winter swimmers experienced improved antioxidant protection compared with the healthy control group. The researchers concluded that the physiological changes observed in the swimmers were indeed the result of regular winter swimming, and that these changes, which they describe as a 'non-damaging form of mild oxidative stress', were responsible for the improved antioxidative protection (Siems et al. 1999: 197).[2]

Siems and colleagues suggest, more speculatively, that life in the affluent west is characterised by a deficiency of natural stimulating factors, such as physical exercise and thermal stimuli, and that this deficiency may contribute to medical problems such as degenerative diseases of the skeletal and muscle systems, heart diseases and infectious diseases (Siems et al. 1999: 193). They argue that the negative results of this deficiency of natural stimuli can partly be prevented by exercise and by body hardening.

The comparative studies of German swimmers indicate that there may be some basis for the belief that regular swimming in cold water has beneficial health effects. In Germany many people swim regularly in lakes and rivers throughout the year. In this country winter swimming is more unusual, and it is hard to believe that many of us would want to undertake this particular form of body hardening in the hope that we might improve our health. Most open-water swimmers will want to wait for summer and somewhat warmer waters, and even then swimming may not necessarily be a vigorous, repeated exercise.

Exercise and health

In considering the possible health benefits of swimming in lakes and rivers, therefore, we are not just talking about hardy regulars who swim, however briefly, all the year round. Nor are we necessarily talking about athletic swimmers who train regularly and seriously and may swim for lengthy periods. Open-water swimming includes everything from splashing about a shallow pool, floating dreamily in a warm lake on a summer evening, or swimming vigorously but briefly across a mountain tarn. Research into the health effects of regular winter swimming or regular competitive swimming is not likely to be as relevant as research into the benefits of exercise more generally, and particularly the benefits of low-impact exercise in the open air and in rural surroundings.

There is considerable evidence that physical exercise of almost any kind can reduce the risks of illness and help in the recovery from illness and accidents. In introducing the Department of Health's overview of the extensive research on the relationship between exercise and health, Sir Liam Donaldson, the Chief Medical Officer at that time, concluded that regular exercise is as important for good health as a healthy diet and not smoking (Department of Health 2004: 1).

A large body of research now indicates that exercise is effective in reducing mortality from a variety of causes, including coronary heart disease, stroke, colon and breast cancer, and heart attacks. It helps to reduce blood pressure and hypertension, and protects against the development of type 2 diabetes. It is a important in preventing obesity, which is associated with a variety of serious health problems. Weight-bearing activities help to maintain bone-mineral density and reduce the risk of osteoporosis. Physical activity also helps to improve balance, coordination and endurance in older people. It plays an important role in enabling people to manage chronic conditions, such as asthma and arthritis. Exercise has psychological benefits, which include bolstering self-esteem, reducing anxiety and stress and enhancing mood. It is effective in treating depression, even severe clinical depression, and promoting good sleep (Department of Health 2004). It has also been found to enhance creativity (Steinberg *et al.* 1997). In addition, the Department of Health's survey concluded that the benefits of moderate exercise far outweighed the risks of injury, although the authors acknowledge that any assessment of risks is hampered by inadequate information on the numbers of people taking part in different activities (Department of Health 2004: 73).

Being out-of-doors

It has long be known that we need to spend time out-of-doors, if for no other reason than to allow sunlight to boost the vitamin D levels in our bodies. There is, however, some evidence – though not nearly so well-established as the evidence on exercise – that simply being out-of-doors in the countryside, or even in urban parks, can bring other benefits for our physical and mental health. In a recent wide-ranging review of the research Jules Pretty and colleagues at the University of Essex argue that two of the primary determinants of physical and mental health, diet and physical activity, are complemented by the secondary roles played by 'connections to nature and to social communities' (Pretty, Griffin *et al.* 2003: 5). They argue that 'closeness to nature' not only increases our sense of well-being but also, disconnections from nature are harmful to individuals and to societies and cultures at large.

DUBS AND TARNS IN THE LAKE DISTRICT

Harry Griffin, who for over half a century wrote about the Lake District in the *Guardian's* 'Country Diary', recalled how he and his friends, when young and fit, used 'to make it a point of honour to bathe in a lake or tarn every weekend – no matter what time of the year' (Griffin 1974: 140). Even young Harry and his friends must have found it hard to summon up courage take a dip on the days when snow lay deep on the Lakeland fells, but there would have been no problem in finding a lake or tarn in which to do so, for nowhere else in England can you find such a variety of routes to walk or places to bathe.

I know of no estimates of the number of tiny deep pools or dubs in the fast-flowing becks where one can slip in for a refreshing dip, if not a swim. But two Grasmere men, Colin Dodgson and Timothy Tyson, claim that there are 463 tarns and that they have swum in all of them (Johnson 2004: 3). Tarns come in many shapes and sizes; some are big, gloomy and uninviting even on the sunniest of days, but there are many tiny sparkling patches of water to delight walkers and tempt one to swim. Stickle Tarn under the glowering cliffs of Pavey Ark (an old reservoir dammed to supply water for the former gunpowder works in the Langdale valley) is not inviting, nor Grizedale Tarn, lying stark and open beside the well-worn path up to Helvellyn. The joy is to find a hidden tarn, just deep enough for a few strokes, and then a comfortable rock, away from passing walkers, on which to sit and dry in the sun.

The Lake District artist, Heaton Cooper, recalls a day when he and his children swam in Easedale Tarn and then climbed up to the smaller, less-visited Codale Tarn where they swam again from the rounded and glaciated rock on the north end and, while he sketched, the 'young people pootled about in the stream, making dams and harbours and racing their stick-boats' (Cooper 1983: 173). Then they made their way home over the ridge to the north and down into Far Easedale. Would that all our children could have the chance to enjoy days like that.

This belief in the restorative effects of exercise taken in the open air, and particularly in inspiring landscapes, is widely shared; it was even cited by the government in bringing forward the 'right to roam' legislation.[3] There is much anecdotal evidence to support these beliefs but, of course, it is not easy to prove or disprove. Now, however, a growing number of researchers from many disciplines are investigating whether contacts with other animals and plants can improve mental and physical health. Roger Ulrich has summarised a large body of research which suggests that leisure activities in natural settings are important in helping people cope with stress, although he accepts that it is less clear how far this holds across diverse groups of people as many studies have used self-selected samples of recreationists (Ulrich 1993). A more recent overview of relevant studies, mainly correlational rather than causal, also suggested that contacts with other animals and plants, fine landscapes and wilderness areas, can improve well-being (Frumkin 2001 and 2002). For some people the psychological benefits appear to be enhanced by exercise that involves physical hardship and a sense of adventure (Herzog *et al.* 2002). Researchers are also beginning to explore the physiological basis for such beneficial effects. There is some evidence that the level of serotonin, a neurotransmitter that can affect our sense of well-being, rises when we are out-of-doors. Exercise can increase the level of serotonin and other neurotransmitters such as beta-endorphin but, we are warned, it is not clear which are responsible for improving mood (Biddle and Mutrie 1991: 190-192). Though the mechanisms that link physical activity and mood are not yet understood, and though the beneficial effects of exercise taken in the countryside may not be experienced by everyone and in all cultures, here, in this urbanised island, the great outdoors appears to have powerful restorative effects for many people.[4]

Walking is, of course, the key to the countryside. It is by far the most popular form of outdoor exercise and one of the healthiest and safest. Roy Shephard, in summarising various controlled longitudinal studies of walking programmes, concludes that these demonstrate that walking increases aerobic fitness, brings modest reductions in blood pressure, improves lipid profiles, increases bone density and enhances mood (Shephard 1997). Walking for pleasure, being both healthy and relatively risk-free, appears to have the best benefit-to-risk ratios of all spare-time activities (Ball 1998). For many wild swimmers, swimming in lakes and rivers is closely associated with walking, particularly in upland areas where many of the best opportunities for such swimming can be found. In the Lake District, that paradise for walkers and wild swimmers, a dip in a tarn is quintessentially part of a walk, sometimes the purpose of the walk, but more often a brief but delightful interlude in a much longer walk across the fells (see box 'Dubs and Tarns in the Lake District').

It's good to laugh

Unlike pedalling an exercise bicycle or keeping pace with a treadmill in an earnest attempt to lose weight or get fit, we walk and swim in the open air because we enjoy it. Though many people may think them masochistic, even winter swimmers swim because they love it and enjoy the feeling of exhilaration that follows. For many of us, like Jack Overhill who is reputed to have swum in the river Cam every day for 62 years, that is enough. But enjoyment also appears to be an important element in good health. It has long been widely believed that enjoyment and laughter are important contributors to health and well-being. Again we don't appear to have much hard evidence, for research into the effects of happiness and laughter upon health is at a very early stage and the direction of any causal links are unclear (Provine 2000). But there is evidence that positive thinking can have direct effects on heart beat variability and be helpful in reducing blood pressure and controlling stress , and that laughter may be good for the immune system. Happy people tend to be healthier and live longer (Layard 2004: 23-24).

The authors quoted in the first chapter demonstrate the power of swimming in lakes and rivers to change their mood and uplift their spirits, and not just while they are swimming. Memories of a good swim or good swimming places can bring back these life-enhancing thoughts. This may help to keep them healthier. Certainly it makes them happier, and that would seem to be sufficient reason why public authorities should take seriously the aspirations of those who wish to swim in natural waters. Enabling more people to do so may also bring wider benefit for the environment. We look at these in the next chapter.

11

TREAD LIGHTLY, SWIM GENTLY – SWIMMING AND THE ENVIRONMENT

… how to be alive
in all this gazed-up on and cherished world
and do no harm

John Burnside 'History' in *The Light Trap* 2002

We could never have loved the earth so well if we had had no childhood in it
George Eliot *The Mill on the Floss* 1860: 69

Sustainability is the buzzword in public-policy documents today. They begin with a genuflection to this elusive concept regardless of how far the following paragraphs attempt to translate it into policy. Though the concept is an elastic one, often stretched to cover any social, economic or environmental improvement, it sometimes encompasses a concern to encourage people to adopt more environmentally friendly lifestyles and this should include how they use their leisure time.

In this chapter we look at the impact of swimming on the environment, and how it impinges upon other people enjoying the countryside, and compare this with the impact of other leisure pursuits, especially water-based sports and pastimes. We also explore the synergies between promoting good conditions for open-water swimming and other changes that benefit the environment. And we consider whether taking part in quiet, non-motorised activities in the countryside, such as walking and swimming, engenders an emotional affinity with the natural world, an affinity that encourages us to take action to protect the environment.

The impact of outdoor recreation

All human activities affect the environment, for good or ill, in a multitude of ways, though such impacts are usually little understood and difficult to evaluate. We noted in chapter 5 that countryside planners, influenced by landowning and conservation interests, used to regard recreational pressures as the major threat to the countryside environment. We now realise that it has been modern agricultural operations, including land drainage, over-grazing and the use of herbicides and pesticides, that have caused the most harm to the countryside and its wildlife (Curry 1994).

Nevertheless, people seeking their recreation in the countryside, particularly those engaged in motorised sports, do have undesirable impacts on the environment, and they may also harm or cause annoyance to other people. The increasingly popular four-wheel drive vehicles can damage fragile vegetation, create noise and disturbance which seriously interferes with the enjoyment of the countryside users, and cause pollution, locally and globally, by burning fossil fuels. Even the low-key activities, the 'quiet enjoyment' such as walking and picnicking that are so favoured and promoted by countryside planners, have some unwanted effects. Picnickers may leave litter, such as ring-pulls of drink cans, that can harm animals. Their dogs may disturb ground-nesting birds or worry sheep. Walkers can cause severe, though localised, erosion of popular routes which, especially in upland areas, may require expensive repairs.

Water-based pursuits have a variety of harmful effects, through pollution and disturbance, on certain plant and animal species, as well as on the enjoyment of other people. Again it is the motorised sports that do the most damage. The wash from motorboats, particularly when they are travelling fast, can seriously erode river banks. It has been estimated that water-skis and speedboats cause four times as much damage by their wash as canoes and kayaks (Liddle 1997: 499). Motorboats can also pollute the water with oil and petrol. The noise of water-skiers or jet-skiers on a mountain lake can destroy the sense of being away from it all for many other people for miles around. Cruisers can discharge raw sewage into rivers, despite the Environment Agency's provision of pump-out facilities for sewage. And all motorised craft contribute to air pollution and global warming. Yet while the agency has, until recently, discouraged swimming and still does little for swimmers, it is encouraging more boats to use the waterways – although it intends, through its charging policy and provision of facilities, to favour electric-powered boats and non-motorised craft (Environment Agency n.d.(b)).

The Environment Agency, as we saw in chapter 4, not only puts considerable resources into improving conditions for angling, but also encourages people to take up the sport. In an advertisement in our local newspaper, designed to encourage more people to take up angling, the head of the agency's fisheries argued that by so doing they 'could easily improve the quality of their lives and the quality of the environment' (Environment Agency 2003). It may do the former, but not necessarily the latter. Although the agency's work to improve conditions for fish certainly does have important beneficial spin-offs for the environment, the activity of angling can have detrimental effects on wildlife. Lead poisoning of swans has become less of a problem in recent years since most anglers now use non-lead weights, but discarded nylon line and hooks still ensnare swans and other water birds. Angling can also pollute water bodies through increasing the concentration of bacteria in them (English Nature 1998). Studies in the Broads have indicated that maintaining fishing there inhibits efforts to restore the water clarity and the biodiversity that was once a characteristic of these lakes.[1] In addition, various management practices designed to improve opportunities for anglers to catch fish can damage the ecology of rivers and lakes. Stocking with desired fish, introducing alien species and removing unwanted species, can harm native fish species through competition and disease. Modifications to lakes or river banks for the convenience of anglers can also damage the riparian ecology (Maitland 1995).

In addition to these undesirable ecological effects, angling – especially coarse fishing – raises the wider ethical problem of the suffering it causes to the fish when they are caught. Peter Maitland, a leading authority on fresh-water fish, comments that:

> Fish are vertebrates and as such are clearly included in the Animals (Scientific Procedures Act 1986 (Home Office 1990); the objective of this Act is to control the scientific procedures applied to an animal 'which may have the effect of causing that animal pain, suffering, distress or lasting harm'. Thus no scientist can carry out any potentially painful experiment on a vertebrate without an appropriate licence and approval for the work involved … An experiment involving impaling live fish on hooks and then leaving them in the water for extended periods would definitely come within the Act and probably would only be allowed under anaesthetic. Yet in the wild, anglers consign thousands of fish every year to a painful and lingering death… (Maitland 1995: 451).

Such practices could be banned with little effect on angling, and well-run clubs, such as Henleaze Angling Club which shares the Henleaze swimming lake, already forbid many of them.[2]

Swimmers cause no such suffering, though they may cause some localised damage and disturbance. Swimmers, like walkers and picnickers, can trample vegetation at the water's edge. On entering the water they may, by stirring up bottom sediments, increase the turbidity of rivers and lakes. As organisms from the faeces of warm-blooded animals concentrate and persist in the sediments, such disturbance can release pathogens into the water and thus, temporarily, reduce water quality. But these effects tend to be short-lived and localised. Michael Liddle, in a comprehensive work on the ecological impacts of outdoor recreation, concludes that the effects of swimming are insignificant by comparison with other water sports, except where they are particularly concentrated in space and time (Liddle 1997: 495). Of all the water-based recreational activities, swimming in lakes, rivers or the sea is among the most benign (Maitland and Morgan 1997). However, like any other leisure activity, it becomes much less benign if we have to make a long car journey to find a good place to swim.

By contrast, if we swim in conventional swimming pools, where we are frequently being advised to swim, we contribute to pollution in various ways. Swimming pools, particularly indoor pools, cause environmental damage through the energy that is used in their construction, the energy expended in heating and lighting the buildings and the water, with pool temperatures around 29° C to 30° or even higher now common, as well as the continuous use of disinfecting chemicals.

Competing for space

Although some recreational users of inland waters have relatively little adverse effects upon the aquatic system, they are sometimes competing for limited space and may cause disturbance to other people wishing to enjoy the water or the land around. The University of Brighton study, discussed in chapter 9, found that such conflicts tend to be greatest between fishermen and canoeists (University of Brighton 2001: para. 9.6). In most cases, however, conflicts between users can be resolved by zoning.

Swimmers, too, can cause disturbance to fishermen, just as fishing lines can get in the way of bathers. Concern to ensure that swimmers do not interfere with the interests of fishing was, as we saw earlier, one of the reasons why Wessex Water does not allow swimming in its reservoirs. But most swimmers are not seeking large areas of water space, and swimmers can easily be separated from other lake users by a line of buoys, as at Frensham Great Pond, so that they do not get in the way of sailing boats and the boats don't endanger the swimmers. Swimmers and anglers, too, can share even quite small stretches of water; they do so to mutual advantage in the Henleaze lake (see box on page 83). Generally, swimmers pose few problems for people taking part in other water-based activities.

Common interests

Not only does swimming pose little threat to the environment and cause minimal nuisance to other water or waterside users, there are important synergies between promoting good conditions for open-water swimming and other environmental improvements. Measures to improve water quality, maintain flows or restore rivers to more natural conditions in the interests of flood control or wildlife, can often benefit bathers. Conversely, measures that would make rivers or lakes more attractive for bathing, by improving water quality or the adjacent landscape, would benefit other countryside users such as walkers and picnickers, anglers and canoeists. They could also bring significant benefits for wildlife.

Most water users need, or at least would like to have, relatively unpolluted water. In this respect they all gain from the work of the Environment Agency in working to improve the quality of river water in England and Wales. The agency's water-quality objectives have reflected the interests of domestic water supplies, fisheries and wildlife, but the improvements that follow have benefited many other water users. The agency now recognises that swimming is a legitimate use of rivers but, in drawing up its river-basin management plans, does not appear to take into account those places where, informally, people do swim. Were it to do so, the benefits would be widely shared. The designation of coastal bathing beaches required improvements to our sewage-disposal infrastructure and resulted in significant improvements in water quality around the coast, increasing the pleasure of many other users of our beaches and coastal waters. Recognising that people swim in rivers would bring similar benefits to us all.

There would be additional costs but the gains, being so widely shared, would be likely to outweigh the additional costs. Jules Pretty and colleagues at the University of Essex, for example, have recently attempted to assess the costs of freshwater eutrophication, the problems caused by the excessive enrichment of water with nitrogen and phosphates which can cause algal blooms. They estimated that the total cost (which ranged from the direct costs to the water companies in treating drinking water to the more uncertain effects on wildlife, recreation and amenity) were in the region of £75 to £114 million a year in England and Wales.[3] This far outweighed the estimated £55 million that is currently being spent on counter-acting the problem. They conclude that, in common with other environmental problems, it would be cost effective if these losses were prevented at source (Pretty, Mason et al. 2003). The beneficiaries could include swimmers, were they allowed to use the lakes, who would be relieved of the need to be wary of blue-green algae. Adding swimmers to the potential users strengthens the argument for tackling such problems at source.

Another shared interest among river users is the maintenance of steady river flows. The idea of maintaining steady flows, in the interest of fisheries and to dilute sewage and industrial effluent, has been a principle of river management since the nineteenth century. It was not until the late twentieth century that river managers began take into account the interests of nature conservation, and to a lesser extent aesthetics and recreation, balancing these interests against the demands for water consumption. Building these wider objectives into the plans for river management is important for all who use rivers or enjoy riverside areas, including river swimmers. Were the Environment Agency to take the interests of swimmers into account, in suitable stretches of river, this would give yet another reason for maintaining steady river flows.

Likewise, there are many potential beneficiaries of current moves towards 'softer' approaches to river engineering. We noted in chapter 3 how modifications to rivers, in the interests of land drainage or to ease local flood problems, have often degraded the landscape, adversely affected wildlife, and made them less attractive or less accessible for swimming. Recent experience in restoring some rivers to a more natural state indicates that it is possible to achieve effective flood control as well as protecting wildlife and improving the landscape, with obvious benefits for public enjoyment. It is now recognised that hard-engineering measures, such as canalisation and culverting, are not always the best solution to flood problems. In some cases a softer engineering approach is not only effective but also reduces the costs of maintenance (RSPB et al. 1994). Use of vegetation to protect river banks from erosion by boat wash can prove more cost-effective than hard edges (Murphy et al. 1995). The re-establishment of trees and hedges on river banks can help to control the growth of weeds in rivers, can benefit fish and increase the numbers and diversity of invertebrates, as well as reducing bank erosion. Flood-relief channels can be designed to leave existing fine rivers undisturbed. Jeremy Purseglove, an ecologist with much experience of working with river engineers, describes such a scheme for the river Blithe in Staffordshire. A dry channel was excavated through grazing land for winter flood-relief, leaving the main river, much prized by fishermen for its magnificent chub, unspoilt. The scheme left undisturbed the fine sequence of pools and riffles in the main river that supported alternating colonies of water lilies and water crowfoot, as well as a deep pool by the bridge that was very popular with bathers (Purseglove 1988: 181).

The more natural-looking riverscapes that result from such new approaches to river engineering are also more attractive for walking and picnicking than heavily engineered rivers. The motivation behind much of the river work of this kind is to improve conditions for fish to spawn. River restoration works may include installing riffles by using stones and coarse gravel to create shallower stretches over which the water flows faster, and retaining or excavating pools in places where the river tends naturally to deepen. The variations in depth and water speed encourage biological diversity. The pools provide the depth needed for water lilies to flourish, and good conditions for adult fish and sometimes for bathers. Yet again, were the Environment Agency to add the interests of swimmers to the considerations to be taken into account in river restoration, it would add to the benefits of such schemes and to the reasons for them to be extended.

Enjoyment and commitment

For many years nature conservation and public access were seen as being in conflict. Nature reserves, typically small intensively managed areas, were often accessible only to trust members or by special permit. In recent years there has been a change in approach. Helped by substantial grants from the lottery and landfill-tax distributors, conservation organisations such as the county wildlife trust and the Woodland Trust, have been able to begin acquiring larger areas and opening them up more widely to the public. These acquisitions coincide with the beginnings of a change in approach, from intensive management of small areas to less intensive management of large areas where there is more scope for natural processes to operate. The two projects in the Fens, featured in the box on page 25, demonstrate this change of approach. At the same time conservation bodies have become increasingly aware that they need public support. They now believe that if people can be allowed to explore their nature reserves and learn more about wildlife and ecology, they are more likely to support conservation activities.

Conservation organisations and many conservationists now see it as vitally important that children are given a chance not only to learn about natural history, through exploration and discovery, but to enjoy doing so. Although we may feel that this must be true, there has been little empirical research to test such beliefs. What has been done, however, suggests that playing or walking in natural surroundings, and experiencing the natural world with all the five senses, are more effective than acquiring a formal knowledge of natural history or an awareness of environmental problems (Finger 1994, Palmer 1998 , Kals *et al.* 1999). Kals and colleagues found that an 'emotional affinity with nature' – which they describe as encompassing such emotions as 'feeling good, free, safe in nature, and a feeling of oneness with nature' – was as powerful in predicting protective behaviour as a more academic interest in nature.

Many open-water swimmers, as the writers quoted in the first chapter testify, experience the sort of emotions described by Kals and his colleagues when they are swimming. Such swimmers are certainly more completely exposed to the elements of the natural world than most people enjoying the countryside. Although some swim all the year round, for many of us wild swimming is essentially a seasonal activity – a celebration of summer. Wild swimmers feel the seasons – the winds and the rain, the sun and the cool water – and come as close to the natural world as it is possible to get. This may, perhaps, help them to be more sensitive to the threats to it.

12

LET'S GO OUT TO SWIM – MAKING IT POSSIBLE

... beside our springs
Sit down, and in our mossy valleys, on
Some bank beside a river clear, throw thy
Silk draperies off, and rush into the stream:
Our valleys love the Summer in his pride.

William Blake *To Summer*

The man who is swimming against the stream knows the strength of it
Woodrow Wilson *The New Freedom* (1913)

Our well-watered land is threaded with streams and rivers and bejewelled with lakes and ponds. It is a marvellously varied countryside, despite the ravages of recent farming and forestry, reflecting its complicated geology and millennia of manipulation and adaptation by man. Many of our rivers and lakes would make delightful places to bathe; many are clean enough for us to do so without endangering our health; some are dangerous but others are relatively safe. Over the centuries many people have enjoyed swimming in these waters. Fewer do so now than 50 years ago, but more would like to do so – could they be reassured about pollution and could they find good places where they are clearly allowed to swim. Yet, as we have documented here, public authorities in England and Wales have, in recent years, increasingly discouraged or prohibited people from swimming in these waters.

We have seen that attitudes to freshwater swimming have fluctuated over the centuries. Whereas in the sixteenth century it met with disapproval, in the late nineteenth and early twentieth centuries local authorities gave river swimmers practical support. It is time for the pendulum to swing back again. Previous chapters have set out the case for public policy to recognise the legitimacy of swimming in lakes and rivers and, in suitable places, to encourage it: a case that rests upon the value of the activity both to individuals and also to society. Though swimming entails some risks, it is not nearly as dangerous as we have been led to believe; the rewards, in terms of happiness and well-being, are great. Swimming causes little harm to other people or to the environment, and there are potential synergies between making lakes and rivers better for swimming and other environmental improvements. And we have some reason to believe that people who find their enjoyment close to the natural world develop a commitment to care for it.

There are many practical measures that public authorities could take to enable people to find places, near to their homes, where they could swim, as well as things that swimmers could do to help themselves. We look at these before considering the longer term legal changes that are needed if we are to gain the freedom to swim in lakes and rivers.

Swimming in existing lakes

Except in the Lake District and parts of Wales, we are not endowed with many natural lakes. Most of our lowland lakes are artificial. Some are relics from the excavation of peat, stone, sand or gravel. Others were created as fishponds, hammer ponds, ornamental lakes in the grounds of country houses, reservoirs to provide water for canals, hydraulic power or drinking water. Lakes, as we saw in chapter 8, often have better quality water than rivers and some lakes are cleaner than some popular sea beaches. Although we only have nine inland sites designated as official bathing places in England and Wales, many large water bodies contain sufficiently low levels of microbiological contamination that they would comply with the Bathing Water Directive. In summer shallow lakes warm up more quickly than the sea. Although some may be weedy or have underwater obstructions, they are usually free from the strong currents which can make rivers and sea beaches dangerous. Yet so few of our lakes are available for swimming.

Where such lakes form part of publicly owned land, such as country parks, this situation could easily be changed. Country parks, which were set up to give opportunities for people to enjoy informal countryside activities within easy reach of their homes, often contain lakes but, as we saw in chapter 5, swimming is usually forbidden in them. In some cases where bathing used to take place it was curtailed when the park became formally designated. In other cases, swimming was allowed for a while but has since become prohibited. Not all lakes, of course, were suitable for swimming, at least not without some modification such as grading the shore lines or removing large underwater obstructions. But some, like the lake at Black Park, were good for swimming, with clear water and shallow edges (see box on page 51).

Gone are the days when local authorities allowed people to swim free of charge and provided lifeguards to watch over them. The Corporation of London, however, continues to be a notable exception. The three very popular ponds on Hampstead Heath, owned and maintained by the corporation, are supervised by lifeguards and bathing is free, although voluntary contributions are requested to help with the costs of maintenance and improvements. This arrangement, however, is under review. Most local authorities are not so well-off as the Corporation of London, but there may be scope for bringing in income at popular locations. At the children's

A LOVELY SANDY BEACH FOR KIDS

Bathers and picnickers at Frensham Great Pond have the medieval monks, as well as Waverley Borough Council, to thank for a lovely place to spend a sunny summer's day. Frensham Great Pond, like its smaller sister pond, was dug in the late twelfth or early thirteenth century as a fishpond, and records suggests that they were very productive in supporting bream, pike and three or four hundred other sorts of fish (Steane 1988: 57). The smaller lake is now an SSSI and not considered suitable for swimming, but the larger lake is one of the nine inland bathing beaches in England and Wales designated under the EC Bathing Water Directive.

The Great Pond lies within a large expanse of heathland, just south of Farnham in Surrey, owned by the National Trust and managed by Waverley Borough Council as a country park for the benefit of wildlife and recreation. A large expanse of soft, golden sand slopes down to a gently shelving and relatively warm lake, where two areas are cordoned-off for bathing. It is ideal for young children to run in and out of the water in safety. Lifeguards used to be provided at peak times, but now people swim at their own risk. Prominent notices warn people of the dangers and, following a fatal accident a few years ago, inflatables are banned. Bathers must keep within the area defined by buoys, to avoid getting in the way of sailing boats and to ensure that the boats do not endanger bathers. Here, as at many well-managed coastal beaches, the emphasis is on banning dogs, which are not allowed in the beach area, rather than banning swimmers. The defined bathing areas are more generous than at the Cotswold Country Park and, although the lake may not be very exciting for adults, it is an excellent place for children to have fun and perhaps to learn to swim.

A charge is made for car parking at weekends and bank holidays, and some income comes from the cafe to help off-set management costs. Park managers estimate that the site receives about 200,000 visitors a year. Some come just to sunbathe on the beach, but for those who wish to swim, the lake provides good-quality water and a safer environment than many a seaside beach.

beach in the Cotswold Country Park, where lifeguards are provided, the charges for car parking and the income from the cafe go a significant way towards off-setting the costs of management and supervision.

The public purse is currently being squeezed hard, and local authorities, in particular, are finding it difficult to find the money for their discretionary activities. But when our society comes to believe again in the importance of public expenditure on social goods, as surely it will, then we should expect local authorities to allocate some funds to make suitable lakes more accessible and, if necessary, safer and more attractive for swimmers, and even perhaps to provide peak-time super-vision of swimming at popular locations. Now that local and national strategies put great emphasis upon 'sustainability' and 'social inclusion', there should be some money for this healthy, environmentally friendly activity that can be enjoyed by people of all ages and abilities.

Making new lakes suitable for swimming

We are creating new lakes all the time, particularly in lowland England, through the extraction of sand, gravel and other minerals. Local authorities could ensure that some of these, in accessible locations, were at least made suitable for swimming. Such lakes are usually in private ownership and therefore local author-ities cannot prescribe precisely how they will be used. But they can, through their planning powers, determine broadly how the land may be used after the extraction and how the lakes and the landscape around them are restored. Increasingly, flooded pits are being allowed to remain and developers are being encouraged to restore them as wildlife reserves, or for fishing or other forms of recreation. In such cases planning authorities sometimes require the shorelines to be bulldozed to create a series of sheltered bays and more exposed headlands, the lake margins in the bays to be reprofiled to create more gentle gradients to encourage the estab-lishment of marginal vegetation or to accommodate fishing platforms and bird hides, and the surrounding land to be landscaped and made suitable for walking, cycling and picnicking. It is open to the local authority to suggest that, in addition to making the lake better for wildlife or fishing, developers should create a gently shelving beach giving easy access to the water, where a swimming area could be demarcated. Where a lake remains in private hands the potential swimming area could then be leased to a local swimming club, or it could be acquired by the local authority or a trust and managed as a public facility within an otherwise commer-cial water park.

In this way the needs of swimmers could be built into plans for the restoration of mineral workings. But in this country this seldom, if ever, happens. Nor do we seem to have any guidance on how to select or adapt suitable sites for swimming, as they do, for example, in the United States.[1] The extraction of sand and gravel in the extensive Cotswold Water Park is now being controlled to ensure that the exca-vated areas will be suitable for water sports, although this does not include swimming. The small children's beach at Cotswold Country Park (discussed in chapter 9) occupies part of one lake that was created before this policy was in place, but it demonstrates the potential for deliberately creating beaches and swimming areas as part of the planned extraction process.

Improving water quality in lakes

Although lakes tend to have better water quality than rivers, when enriched with nitrogen and phosphorus they are susceptible to algal blooms in hot weather, just when swimmers most want to swim. This is often cited as a reason, or an excuse, to ban swimming, not just when the blooms occur but at all times. The Environment Agency's Aquatic Weeds Research Unit developed a technique using barley straw, which counteracts blue-green algae effectively, cheaply and without any undesirable side effects. It has been used as the solution at the Cotswold Country Park and Henleaze Swimming Club. Henleaze found that barley straw sausages, costing just £27.50, kept the water in the lake clear throughout the five-month swimming season. Recently, however, they have come to the conclusion that this method of control is not worth the effort involved. A simpler solution is to rake the strands out of the water. At Frensham Great Pond, which also occasionally suffers from algae and pond weed being blown towards the bathing area, the managers simply ban swimming briefly until they can clear it away.[2]

Algal blooms may result in temporary closure of a lake to swimmers, but they seldom justify a permanent ban. Sometimes, however, lakes may be affected by more serious pollution requiring expensive and specialised treatment. In the case of designated bathing waters the Environment Agency has the responsibility not only to identify the source of the pollution, but also to work to secure a remedy. In seeking to improve the water at Millerground, one of the three designated bathing waters on Lake Windermere, the agency used a DNA identification technique to identify the many different causes of pollution. The subsequent remedial action included by-laws prohibiting the discharge of sewage to the lake, improvements to sewage treatment works including removal of nutrients to inhibit algal blooms, plans to deal with storm water overflows, a campaign to reduce run-off from farm-land, and measures to control discharges into the lake from hotels and caravan parks. This demonstrates how designating more sites as bathing waters could be an important way to secure better water quality for bathers and other water users.[3]

Creating 'natural' swimming pools

The technique of using plants to cleanse water is so effective that domestic waste water, including sewage, can be made clean enough for swimming. An innovative low-impact housing development at Hockerton near Nottingham, designed by the pioneering architects Robert and Brenda Vale, uses aquatic plants to cleanse the waste water from the houses. The effluent sewage is initially treated in a septic tank, the overflow from which goes into a large pond with a series of floating rush mats on which reeds (*phragmites communis*) and mace grow. These mats are arranged with baffles to form a spiral through which the waste water flows. The treatment pond is at the upper end of a large lake, specially constructed for the project, and the water from the pond flows into the lake. The lake was designed to attract wildlife and appears to have been successful in doing so, but it also provides the residents with their own outdoor swimming pool with water quality that meets the Bathing Water Directive's higher (guideline) standard for bathing beaches. The designers at Hockerton have ingeniously turned a nasty problem – sewage – into a visual, social and ecological amenity.[4]

There are now a number of commercial firms offering so-called 'natural' swimming pools for private gardens using plants, rather than chemicals, to treat the water. This technology has been widely used in Germany, Switzerland and Austria. Such 'natural' swimming pools offer a greener alternative to conventional swimming pools, with good quality water that can be enjoyed by people, frogs and other wildlife, although one is advised not to stock them with fish as this would pollute the water. Though 'natural pools' are slightly cheaper to install and cheaper to maintain than conventional pools, they are likely to be available only to affluent people with large gardens as they require more space than conventional swimming pools with at least one-third of the pond area being set aside for plants. Such pools could, however, be considered in communal areas of new blocks of flats, as part of the arrangements for dealing with surface run-off, which is discussed below. The same technology, of using aquatic plants to cleanse the water of swimming pools, has also been used in Austria to create public pools. The Austrians have demonstrated that, given the willingness to invest in such projects, we could create small swimming lakes for public use, perhaps in town parks, that would blend into the landscape and provide habitats for wildlife.

Sustainable urban drainage and river restoration

The same principles, of using plants to cleanse water, are employed in the techniques now being developed known as sustainable urban drainage systems (SUDs). As we expand our towns and villages we put more of the countryside under hard, impermeable surfaces from which the rainwater flows rapidly into drains, streams and rivers. This not only reduces the amount of water available to replenish the aquifers but also, at times of heavy rain, increases the risk of flooding. Local planning authorities are now encouraging developers to incorporate the SUDs principles into the design of large developments, and a few pioneering schemes have been implemented. These channel the run-off from buildings and roads into newly created watercourses and lakes so that some of the water returns to the rivers more slowly and more of it soaks down into the aquifers.

The streams and lakes, thus created, can be landscaped to provide attractive areas for people and for wildlife. Whereas post-war planners would incorporate lakes into their plans for new towns, with illustrations depicting children paddling and perhaps swimming, illustrations in current plans show, typically, ponds with children feeding the ubiquitous ducks, and no hint that they might be used for swimming. In the new village of Cambourne near Cambridge, however, a village where the interests of wildlife were built into the initial plans, the surface run-off from part of the village was engineered to drain down into two lakes forming part of a new country park.[5] At the head of the higher lake appropriate varieties of aquatic plants were established to cleanse the water flowing into it. This lake was planned and constructed with gently shelving edges and fishing platforms to make it suitable for the villagers to swim and fish, but subsequently the parish council decided it should stop children swimming there, and the usual 'no swimming' notices have appeared. The water in the lake now looks muddy and none too inviting, probably because the area devoted to water-cleansing aquatic plants at its head was much too small. This could easily have been rectified, but instead the council abandoned an unusual and imaginative plan to give the people of Cambourne their local swimming lake.

Just as SUDs schemes could be designed to create lakes suitable for paddling or swimming, so river-restoration schemes could take into account the potential for swimming. The new softer approach to river engineering whereby river restoration schemes are carried out in the interests of flood control, fishing, wildlife conservation or landscape improvement can, as an unplanned benefit, also improve conditions for swimmers. The installation of riffles and weirs, for example, which encourage fish to spawn, will sometimes create deeper pools below them which are good for swimming. The interests of swimmers could, however, be built more directly into such schemes. Were the Environment Agency to give swimmers some of the consideration it gives to anglers, river restoration schemes could be planned so that the newly created pools are located where there is public access along the river banks, or where a footpath or minor road crosses the river, so that people – whether walkers, picnickers or swimmers – could also reach them and enjoy them.

People power

We do not need to leave it just to the authorities. There is much that people could do, working nationally and locally, to regain the freedom to swim in lakes and rivers. Pressure groups have played an important role in helping to improve conditions for coastal swimmers. The Coastal Anti-Pollution League, later incorporated into the Marine Conservation Society, has been instrumental in securing improved water quality, which benefits swimmers and surfers, divers and sailors, as well as marine flora and fauna. The governing bodies of other water sports have secured influence with the authorities responsible for planning and management of water bodies and adjacent land. The British Canoe Union, in its River Access Campaign, has been pressing the case for more access to inland waters, and claims credit for helping to persuade the government to commission the study by the University of Brighton, discussed in chapter 9, which led to a further study on how access agreements might be used to open up more inland waters for water sports.[6] But until recently there was no such body working to promote the interests of inland swimmers. In drawing up the right to roam proposals, the government consulted a large number of organisations, bodies as far removed from inland access issues as the Association of Sea Fisheries and the British Council of Shopping Centres, but no organisation concerned with swimming, not even the long-established Amateur Swimming Association (DETR 1998). Now, however, the River and Lake Swimming Association is working to pursue the interests of swimmers in inland waters, and their voice should be heard in future consultations.

More locally, too, riverside community groups can have a role. Many such groups are already helping to care for their rivers through Anglian Water's River Care Project.[7] Much of their energies tend to be devoted to the very basic task of picking up litter along the banks and, sometimes with the help of canoeists, retrieving shopping trolleys and bicycles from the river. But it does not have to stop there. River Care groups and other community organisations can take practical steps to help protect and improve beauty spots or fragile habitats.

Local volunteers could also restore traditional bathing or paddling places. Although the River Care organisers warn people to stay out of rivers – they tend to be unduly worried about Weil's Disease – local groups can seek grants from a variety of other sources to improve their environment. In Shepreth, a small village near Cambridge, the Friends of the River Shep have for several years been working to improve this tiny tributary of the river Cam. In several places, upstream and downstream of the village, this straightened ditch has been encouraged to flow faster, within a narrower and more sinuous course, by planting willow stakes. Riffles have been created to encourage the brown trout to spawn. In the middle of Shepreth, below the pretty bridge, the river runs shallowly over a gravelly bed. Here the children have long enjoyed paddling and fishing and, as the water is clean, parents have been happy to let them do so. However, over the years the stream silted up a bit and the bank became eroded and muddy. Friends of the River Shep, therefore, constructed a new, stable bank using two substantial wood logs, coir logs and geotextile matting. The work was welcomed by the villagers and the children who play there. Liz Kendrick reports, on behalf of the Friends of the River Shep, that the only health and safety concern she has heard voiced is that of cars speeding through the village – not a whisper about Weil's disease.[8]

In a similar way, local groups could (with the agreement of the landowner and any necessary consents from the Environment Agency or the local authority) restore former bathing places from encroaching vegetation, remove litter and obstructions, keep a check on water quality, and bring any pollution problems to the attention of the agency.

Swimming clubs

Water-skiers, scuba divers, canoeists and, particularly, anglers have gained access to inland waters through organising themselves into clubs to lease rights to use land and water for their sport. Swimmers could also seek to secure rights to use good swimming spots on private lakes or stretches of river, near towns and villages, enabling their members to swim near their homes. Swimming clubs could make an important contribution to extending the opportunities for people to swim and to do so in relative safety. Clubs keep a watch on water quality. At both Henleaze and Farleigh Hungerford, for example, the water is checked regularly and both clubs ban dogs from their sites. The Bristol club takes samples from its lake every two weeks during the swimming season for analysis at the Bristol Public Health Laboratory. Clubs also help to prevent drownings and other accidents through strict club rules and through the informal surveillance by family, friends and other club members. Both Farleigh Hungerford and the Bristol club have rules governing their members' behaviour. The rules at Henleaze are particularly comprehensive and

Above: Bathing above the weir at Farleigh Hungerford, summer 1999 (Photograph: © Rob Fryer)
Right: Boys jumping off Halfpenny Bridge at Lechlade, summer 2003

strict. Here, since the lake has no shallow edges and is often cold, the rules require that club members must be able to swim 50 metres in the lake and the club officials check that they can do so. The club employs several part-time superintendents to ensure, among other things, that the rules are kept. Though two of these are qualified lifeguards, their function is seen as preventing accidents rather than rescuing swimmers, an approach which the club management sees as more appropriate to open waters which lack the clarity of conventional swimming pools. Swimming at Farleigh Hungerford is somewhat less formal, but the club also gives guidance on safety and its rules require that children under 12 are accompanied by their parents.

Swimming clubs, particularly if managed in this way, could also make a broader contribution to water safety. On the warm summer evening that I visited Farleigh Hungerford there were numerous families with small children enjoying the river. Children who learn to swim in the river Frome or the cold deep lake at Bristol will be far better equipped to cope if they choose to swim in, or if they inadvertently fall or are pushed into, open water elsewhere, than those who have known only warm, still swimming pools.

Peter Cornall, head of water and leisure safety at RoSPA, considers that swimming clubs are the appropriate answer to those who would like to swim in lakes and rivers. He suggests that, in remote upland areas, people who swim in lakes and rivers usually know what they are doing and accept the risks. Elsewhere, he argues, people tend to swim on impulse and, unaware of the dangers, blame the authorities when things go wrong. He sees this as a specifically English problem, pointing

out that English people, unlike their continental neighbours, are not used to swimming regularly in rivers and lakes. Potential swimmers in lowland England, says Cornall, should 'band together, not for freedom for everyone, but for freedom for themselves'.[9]

Informal lake and river swimming

There is certainly scope for more swimming clubs, but they are not the whole answer. They do not, as Peter Cornall recognises, offer freedom for everyone. They cannot provide for those who might want a refreshing swim in the course of a country walk, or to sunbathe and swim on a hot day somewhere close to home. Rather, they would reinforce the trend towards a semi-privatised countryside, a trend which would suit many landowners but which conflicts with the aims of bodies, like English Nature and the sports councils, to break down the social barriers that prevent people from enjoying the countryside and taking part in active sports. Bathing is essentially an informal activity, more like walking, picnicking and bird watching than competitive and organised sports. Countryside policy makers and managers refer to these activities as 'quiet enjoyment' of the countryside, activities that they not only accept as legitimate but actively encourage. Should they not also be helping people to enjoy bathing, informally, without having to belong to a club?

Confining swimming to private swimming clubs and restricting opportunities for informal swimming elsewhere would do nothing to deter the casual reckless bather, particularly the drunken youths whose habits of cooling off are, understandably, of concern to the Environment Agency and who account for a major proportion of water-related deaths. The threat of a £20 fine does not deter youngsters from jumping off Halfpenny Bridge into the Thames at Lechlade. While warning notices and measures to prohibit bathing in particularly dangerous places are needed, more widespread bans may be counter-productive. Bans on bathing from relatively safe traditional bathing places are likely to drive people, especially young people, to seek out less suitable places. This is precisely what happened when people were suddenly prevented from swimming from the gently shelving beach in Hatchmere Lake.[10]

There are still lakes, publicly owned or managed, where the managers allow swimming without lifeguards, as the Forestry Commission does near its picnic site beside Llyn Geirionydd (see box page 46), the National Trust at its two bathing sites on Lake Windermere (see box opposite) and Waverley Borough Council at Frensham Great Pond. It is clear now that, provided the lakes present no unusual dangers, and provided the sites are well managed with appropriate warning signs, managers need no longer fear that they are neglecting their duty of care, under civil law, nor run the risk of prosecution by the Health and Safety Executive.

There are many places in rivers – especially in the west country and Wales – where you can swim with the blessing of riparian landowners, or at least without anyone taking steps to stop you doing so. Many are known only to local people with nothing to indicate that one can swim there. The river at Lechlade, however, is an

BATHING IS PERMITTED HERE – BUT WHO KNOWS?

In England and Wales we do not have a right to swim in most lakes and rivers. One might expect, therefore, that where swimming is officially allowed this would be well-signposted so that people looking for a place to swim could find it. One would certainly expect this to be so at one of the rare inland bathing waters designated under the Bathing Water Directive. We have only nine such sites and three of these are on Lake Windermere in Cumbria. One is a private site run by the YMCA. The other two, Millerground Landing and Fell Foot, are owned by the National Trust and open to the public. But how many visitors to the national park know that they can swim there?

Millerground Landing, near Windermere town, can be reached by a footpath from a layby or from Rayrigg Meadows car park nearby. The pay-and-display car park run by South Lakeland District Council has signs to a lakeside path, but no indication that one can bathe in the lake. The path runs down to a narrow stretch of gently shelving beach, with wooden jetties projecting out into the clear water and magnificent views beyond. On a sunny summer's day the presence of local bathers would suggest that it is a good place to swim. But there is little to indicate that it is an official bathing place. The only clue I found was a small photocopied notice on the sailing base building giving the results of the Environment Agency's water-quality checks for the official bathing waters in this area: three on the lake and three on the coast.

Fell Foot is a country park run by the National Trust near the southern tip of the lake. A notice at its entrance lists various facilities and activities available in the park but says nothing about swimming. Visitors seeking somewhere to swim might not want to risk the high car parking charges on the off-chance they could do so here. But if they persist and walk across the manicured lawns that sweep down to the water's edge, they will find a cafe, boats to rent and a bathing area defined by buoys. A notice warns of cold, deep water and currents, and here they are allowed to swim, without lifeguards, at their own risk.

exception. Here the Thames flows brown and wide through the heart of the village and a notice on its bank, instead of saying 'no bathing', says on one side 'WARNING TO BATHERS UNEVEN DEPTH' and on the other side 'NO MOORING'. Motorboats and canoes, swimmers and swans share the river in happy profusion. Even more remarkable, in our land of 'no swimming' notices, is the attitude of Twyford Parish Council in Hampshire. At Compton Lock on the old 'Itchen Navigation', where people have swum for as long as anyone can remember, the parish council has built wooden steps to help people get in and out of the water. No one now expects local authorities to provide springboards, diving towers and changing rooms as they once did at river bathing places. But they could provide steps into the water at suitable spots where they own the land or with the agreement of the landowner and the Environment Agency. There is a delightful place on the river Cam, below the village of Grantchester, much visited by walkers and picnickers and a sprinkling of swimmers, where it is easy to jump into the water but not so easy to get out again. Were the parish council to provide steps into the river here, it would be a cheap and welcome improvement.

The Grantchester spot is well known, but many unofficial bathing places are not. Even at the two official bathing places on Lake Windermere, there are no signposts pointing to where we can swim. Rob Fryer's pioneering directory lists many spots where he and his friends swim, unsupervised and usually unhindered by riparian owners. Not all are ideal, some are dangerous and many are difficult to find (Fryer 2009). Could we look forward, perhaps, to the day when some of the leaflets about walks in the countryside, produced by local authorities, would draw our attention to the good, and relatively safe places, to swim?

Learning to cope with open waters

More opportunities to swim informally and without lifeguards would, as RoSPA argues, mean more people exposed to the dangers of drowning. If we are to extend such opportunities we need to help people, particularly young people, understand the dangers and learn how to cope with natural waters.

Swimming and water safety are required elements in the national curriculum in primary schools at key stage 2 (7 to 10 years) unless the programme has already been completed at key stage 1 (up to 7 years). It is assumed that the instruction will take place in swimming pools, for the guidance to teachers makes no reference to swimming in open waters.[11] There is also an option of including outdoor and adventurous activities at key stages 2 and 3, but again the guidance does not encompass open-water swimming. But, as RoSPA points out, learning to swim in a warm, clear, current-free swimming pool is insufficient preparation for coping with more natural waters, whether they be the sea, lakes or rivers.

Since most accidental drownings occur to people who fall in, rather than those who choose to swim, it would seem important that young people learn to swim and do so in natural waters. This is likely to be a far more effective way of reducing deaths by drowning than prohibiting swimming in relatively safe places. We noted above how swimming clubs have a valuable role to play here. Outdoor adventure courses could also introduce children to the pleasures and the dangers of swimming in lakes and rivers. Yet, though most outdoor education and activity centres offer children a chance to experience a wide range of exciting and potentially dangerous activities, such as climbing, gorge-walking, white-water rafting and caving, they rarely offer open-water swimming. A trawl through the activities listed by 50 outdoor education and activity centres found only one that mentioned swimming and one offering snorkelling, though some boasted an outdoor heated swimming pool. Swimming in open waters is not only a life-enhancing activity that can more readily be enjoyed throughout life than caving or climbing, it is also a potentially life-saving skill. Surely it should have a place in outdoor education?

Outdoor courses, however, can give only brief and occasional tasters of outdoor activities. They can introduce children to the very different conditions of cold lakes or flowing rivers, but not teach them to swim. Safe swimming spots on lowland rivers and lakes, where families can picnic, play and swim regularly, as they can if they live near the sea, probably offer the best opportunities for young people to experience the joy of swimming in comparative safety and learn how to swim in natural waters.

Change in attitudes

There is much that could be done, given the will, to extend opportunities for people to swim. Some of the suggestions made above would require some public expenditure but most do not. What they do require is a change in attitude by those who control the waters. If we are to have many more places like Frensham Great Pond and Lechlade we need to persuade them not only that that the risks of open-water swimming have been exaggerated but also that swimmers, like people taking part in other sports, are prepared to take risks to do the things that they enjoy.[12]

We need a more intelligent and selective policy for the use of inland waters, recognising that lakes and rivers (like our coastal beaches) vary greatly in their suitability for swimming and the dangers they present. We need to extend opportunities to swim where conditions are good, making suitable places safer and more attractive, as well as deterring people from swimming where they are most dangerous. We may not be able to do much to change the habits of those dare-devil youths who seem to be most at risk and account for most drownings. But we could provide opportunities for more responsible bathers, and those who would like to bathe, to do so where the risks of harm appear to be lowest.

The Environment Agency, now that it accepts swimming as a legitimate activity in rivers, could have an important role. It could define in its river basin plans where swimming might be made safer or pleasanter and build this into the water-quality objectives for particular stretches of water. It could also contribute financially to projects that improve conditions for swimmers, in suitable places, just as it does for anglers, canoeists and other river users. And it could let us know where the good swimming places are. We have a long way to go before we are likely to see notices indicating popular swimming places similar to the French 'BAIGNADE NON SURVEILLEE', but we could start to move in that direction now.

A right to swim

Although much could be done relatively cheaply and within existing legal constraints, if we are to make more widespread progress in extending opportunities, we need a right to swim in inland waters. The right to roam provisions of the Countryside and Rights of Way Act (CROW) 2000 gave us, in England and Wales, a legal right of access on foot to stretches of mountain, moor, heath, down and registered common land where they are defined as access land. This enables us to explore some splendid areas of countryside from which we had been excluded, but it does did not give us a right to paddle or swim in the lakes and rivers within these areas. It is an anomaly that we should seek to rectify. We need to campaign for a right to use waters within the access lands in ways that are environmentally benign and compatible with the spirit of the CROW Act. We should be seeking, at least, a right to paddle and swim in the lakes and rivers within such areas and to paddle canoes along the rivers that run through them. The new freedom should be exercised at our own risk and the new rights should be accompanied by a clause to relieve landowners of their duties of care, in the same way that the current legislation removes any liability for injuries to walkers that arise from 'any natural feature of the landscape'. This would be a small, achievable and welcome extension of our rights to enjoy some of our most exciting countryside.

But in large parts of lowland England the new legislation brings little change. Many people still have only limited opportunities to enjoy the countryside near their homes, including the sort of gentle lowland landscapes that many of them prefer to the mountains and moors, and even fewer opportunities to swim in the lakes and rivers within it. Had we been disposed to consider the experience of Norway, Sweden and Finland, we could have had, as Marion Shoard argued so persuasively when the legislation was being drawn up, a more extensive but simpler and more easily understood right to roam: a right to walk almost anywhere on undeveloped land, near our homes, subject to defined exceptions to protect fragile habitats, growing crops and the privacy of homes (Shoard 1999).

In Scotland now we can paddle and swim in most rivers, lakes, canals and reservoirs, as well as to explore them in non-motorised boats. South of the border, with a different legal system and different political climate, this seems an unrealisable dream, but we still need to campaign for similar legislation to give us a right to walk over more of our lowland countryside and to enjoy, in environmentally friendly ways, the lakes and rivers within it. A new right to swim, which should include a right to use non-motorised boats, would also need to be accompanied (as in the access lands) by limitations on the landowners' liability. We would then be able to paddle, swim and canoe in most of the lakes and rivers of England and Wales, accepting the risks of doing so.

In Philippa Pearce's *Minnow on the Say*, published half a century ago, the simple pleasures enjoyed by Adam, David and Becky, as they canoed up the river from their homes, must be for some children today just a charming and nostalgic scene from a story. Many children now are not allowed such freedom, and in many rivers there is still no public right to canoe or swim. They

> did not hurry: they marked down places that would be good for bathing, or for fishing; ancient willow-trees whose fantastic bendings and twistings invited the climber; meadows that might bear mushrooms; reed beds that might hide the nests of moorhen … and there was the darting flight of

turquoise blue, as a kingfisher – the first that Adam and David had ever seen so close – flew out from its fishing-haunt under the mill bridge, and past them. (Pearce 1955: 246)

One day such pleasures may be there for any child to enjoy. One day we may regain the freedom to walk through our land and swim in its lakes and rivers. Then we will have reversed a trend that has eroded an important freedom. We will be able to turn around and swim with the stream.

Postscript to the second edition

In 2003, when I began researching for this book, unbeknown to me, two veteran swimmers were setting up the River and Lake Swimming Association (RALSA) to campaign for more freedom to swim in our inland waters. Rob Fryer, who had already spent years compiling his pioneering Directory of Cool Places, became the association's chairman. Yakov Lev, who led the successful fight to regain Hatchmere Lake for swimmers, took on the job of secretary and website manager. We have to thank these two determined campaigners for significant changes in the attitudes and policies among national organisations that influence the use of inland waters. A sister organisation, the Outdoor Swimming Society, was formed in 2006 which, in addition to organizing swimming events, also campaigns for swimming in all outdoor locations, including in our endangered lidos.

One of RALSA's first targets was the Environment Agency which, following lobbying by Yakov Lev, now recognises swimming as a legitimate use of inland waters. Its former chairman, Sir John Harman explained in a letter to RALSA in 2005 'We aim to raise awareness of the risks, but people then have the freedom to choose what activities they do.' And, more positively William Crookshank, the agency's head of recreation policy at that time, agreed that swimming in rivers was an acceptable activity 'with low impacts on the environment and users'.[1] This change in attitude at the top has yet to be reflected in the agency's policies and spending but, at least, I no longer see in my local paper its summer press releases warning us not to swim in any river, lake or canal.

Another step forward, potentially more significant, was taken when the Health and Safety Executive (HSE) clarified its guidelines on the management of swimming pools. HSG179, the blue book, was the basis for the inspector's advice to Buckinghamshire County Council and contributed to the decision in 2002 to ban swimming in Black Park. Following representations from RALSA, the executive issued a statement making it clear that, in future, the guidelines would only apply to lakes and rivers where operators actively 'encourage' swimming. We understand that 'encourage' has been defined in case law to mean 'incite', and goes beyond 'knowingly allowing' an activity to take place. Site managers could now feel free to let people swim at their own risk in suitable places without fearing that the executive might prosecute them. The HSE, which has its work cut out dealing with serious workplace dangers, has been unfairly blamed for all sorts of 'health and safety' nonsense such as banning conkers in playgrounds. We can hope that it will no longer be used as an excuse to ban swimming.

Perhaps the most significant change, however, has taken place at RoSPA which, a decade ago, was a strident opponent of swimming in all inland waters. Since then, under the guidance of its water safety officer, Peter Cornall, RoSPA has refined its message and now gives sensible advice on how to enjoy swimming more safely in our lakes and rivers, as well as in the sea. Its recent publications concentrate on the more dangerous manifestations of swimming such as tomb stoning, and stress the crucial message: don't drink and swim.

These changes at the national level are only just beginning to trickle down to lakes and rivers. We have not gained many more places to swim, but there are a few welcome changes and some promises. In response to lobbying by swimming activist Robert Asprey, Anglian Water has agreed to provide a swimming area, open to the public and supervised by voluntary lifeguards, at Rutland Water. This could be a useful example for other water companies to follow. Another promise may be realised near Bedford. Planners of the new Bedford River Valley Park took note of feedback from local people and agreed to include a swimming lake. Some commercially run lakes now offer swimming among their attractions, but normally require swimmers to wear wet suits. That is fine for triathlon and competitive swimmers who stay in the water for a long time, but for most of us swimming cocooned in a wetsuit is not wild swimming.

New opportunities in rivers are harder to find. One imaginative scheme has been completed on the southern edge of Cambridge where, next to a large new housing estate, the developers will provide parkland beside the river to be managed by the local wildlife trust for public access. Before this scheme even started Rob Mungovan, South Cambridge District Council's ecology officer, seized upon the possibility of money from the government's Growth Area Fund to improve the riverside and the river. Ditches were widened to keep people away from sensitive wildlife sites such as the bank where kingfishers nest, a wet meadow was created to accommodate seasonal flooding, and parts of the river bank have been re-graded to help people get down to the river to paddle, launch a canoe or swim.

A little way downstream we have another small example of changing attitudes. The Cam Conservators, the navigation authority for the Cam in this area, have bylaws prohibiting daytime swimming in the river except at the bathing places authorised by the conservators. But, until recently, no such places had been authorised. The conservators have now agreed that a two-mile stretch of river above Cambridge can be a bathing place. Regular swimmers there will not notice any change. Much more significant, however, is the decision by the new Canal and River Trust not to maintain the current ban on swimming in the waterways formerly managed by British Waterways. We have been assured that it will only prohibit swimming where a 'risk assessment demonstrates that the risks to the safety of swimmers are unacceptably high and cannot be controlled by taking reasonable precautions.[2] We do not know what this will mean in practice – when functions are moved to a new body the personnel and corporate mindset tend to go with them – but it could be another step towards more freedom to swim.

In the closing decades of the twentieth century academics investigating the behaviour of people visiting the countryside ignored the possibility that they might go for a swim. More recent studies have revealed that outdoor swimming is by far the most popular of water-based recreation in England and Wales. The studies for the UK as a whole fail to distinguish between open waters and open-air pools, although some of the data collected by the Countryside Council for Wales does make this distinction. Studies carried out by Scottish Natural Heritage have also included questions about wild swimming, indicating that even in Scotland's cooler climate, about twice as many people swim in rivers, lochs and the sea as take part in all other water sports.[3]

Natural England, which took over the Countryside Agency's role in promoting countryside recreation, appears to share its predecessor's lack of interest in wild swimming but, in contrast, the Countryside Council for Wales now celebrates the fact that 'the rivers and lakes of Wales are an amazing place to swim; offering beautiful scenery, crystal clean water and a sense of peace and tranquillity'. It is currently consulting on a draft code of conduct for wild swimmers, as well for canoeists and anglers. The draft code enjoins them to respect other people, protect the environment and gives advice on how to enjoy swimming safely.[4]

Whereas the first study by the University of Brighton into the recreational use of inland waters ignored swimmers, the regional water recreation strategies, which it has prepared for the Environment Agency, now include open-water swimming. In these strategies the authors concede that more opportunities are needed for swimmers but they make few practical suggestions about how to meet this demand. Nor is there any sign so far that the agency is prepared to divert some of its spending on angling and boating towards making conditions better for swimmers. At Byron's pool near Cambridge, where the notorious lord used to swim, the agency recently contributed to an expensive project which included creating a sinuous fish pass to enable fish to migrate up the river, and ten fishing platforms for anglers to catch them. A ladder into the river for swimmers, near the new picnic site and well away from the dangerous weir, would have added only a small fraction to the cost of this project.

In contrast to some welcome changes at a national level, much prejudice remains at the local level. Many county fire services still regard swimming in inland waters as an unusually risky and unacceptable activity. In the summer of 2007 when the firemen tried to rescue an experienced river swimmer against his will from the Severn, the Worcester News reported that the operation involved 25 fire fighters, three fire engines and two rescue boats. When the swimmer reluctantly emerged from the water he was arrested and detained under Section 136 of the Mental Health Act, but released two hours later after a doctor declared that there was nothing wrong with him. Further north, in Cheshire, a county of shallow meres and slow flowing rivers which regularly warm up to 20° centigrade or more in summer, the county fire service issued a poster in 2010 warning young people not to swim because they were 'freezing cold'. It alleged that 'most people who drown in open waters are good swimmers'. In fact, no one knows how well victims of drowning could swim, but we do know that only a small proportion of them drown as a result of deliberately going for a swim.

This prejudice, and the fears of litigation, remain entrenched among local authorities. Despite the legal rulings, reported in Chapter 6, which could relieve landowners and operators of the fear of litigation, and despite the clarification by the HSE of the scope of its blue book, and despite the changes in advice by RoSPA, the 'no swimming' notices continue to litter our country parks and similar recreational areas. Swimming is still banned in Bury Lake and Black Park, and even at Brereton Lake, the scene of the Law Lords' landmark ruling. Brereton Country Park has since been renamed as a nature reserve, and the destruction of the lakeside beaches and the blocking of access to the water is cited as an example of good practice in countryside management by a group of organisations concerned with safety in the countryside. The beautiful lake used to attract many swimmers. Now, we are assured that even on the hottest days, it is rare for staff to need to speak to anyone regarding swimming. 'When this does occur,' the managers boast, 'swimmers are quick to leave. In the past swimmers were determined to continue as so many others were also in the water. Now they feel "out of place".'[5] Feeling out of place can be as much a barrier as a 'no swimming' notice – not to enthusiastic trespassers like the late Roger Deakin – but certainly to many of us more hesitant creatures. Several members of my local river swimming club come from 20 miles or more away, even from places with rivers nearby, because they feel that the club is a place where they can swim without being thought odd.

It is not just 'no swimming' notices or the fear of feeling out of place that deter people from enjoying our inland waters. There is still a widespread perception that rivers are too polluted to swim in. A recent survey carried out for the Blueprint for Water, a coalition of conservation organisations concerned to protect rivers and water resources, found that 97 percent of people questioned regarded rivers, ponds and streams as a 'vital part of the countryside', but over half of them would not swim in their local river because they considered it too polluted.[6] This is a misconception that the Environment Agency, now that it no longer opposes river swimming, could help to allay.

The Environment Agency's work in river basin planning, required by the EC Water Framework Directive, should ensure that the water quality in our rivers continues to improve. This is vitally important for swimmers, as for wildlife and other water users. But, although we can expect our rivers to continue to get cleaner, can we be sure there will be enough water? For many decades, in the drier parts of the country, river flows have been declining, and some streams and rivers have dried up completely, as a result of changes in land use and farming practices, and increasing demands for water for domestic use. The general consensus is that our summers are likely to get hotter and drier, with heavier but more erratic winter rain leading to more floods rather than replenishing the aquifers. The pressures on water resources will increase – and that, of course, is a much broader problem which wild swimmers, as others with a concern for the natural environment, need to address. A right to swim in our rivers would not be much use where the water is too shallow to do so.

The prospect of a change in the law that would give everyone a right to enjoy more of our countryside, and give swimmers and users of non-motorised boats a right to explore more of its waters, is as far away as ever. We are still awaiting decision on Douglas Caffyn's thesis that a common law right to take a boat along navigable rivers was lost simply though a mistake in a nineteenth century legal text. His argument is currently being tested in the courts.[7] But, even if that right were to be established, and even if it were deemed to include swimmers, that would do nothing to remove the 'no-swimming' notices from lakes. The British Canoe Union has been campaigning for over a decade for a right of access to rivers for canoeists and swimmers. There has been growing political support for the campaign in Wales where, in 2009, the National Assembly's Petitions Committee described the current situation as 'confusing, untenable and unworkable' and its chair, Val Lloyd, stated that 'we believe there should be the right of non-motorised access to inland water in Wales as there is in Scotland'.[8]

But this call for free and open access to Welsh waters was not endorsed by the National Assembly of Wales. The Assembly's Sustainability Committee, after an extensive inquiry, decided that voluntary access agreements were the way forward, a view that is shared at Westminster. Richard Benyon, the minister responsible, argues that locally agreed, and voluntary, access agreements fit 'very well with the big society agenda' and can give 'access where it is needed and meet the needs of all users and interested parties'.[9] Voluntary access agreements, as the British Canoe Union points out, will not help canoeists for many reasons, not least the difficulties of finding out who owns the land along a river. Such agreements could help a swimming club gain access to a lake or river bank, but promise nothing for casual swimmers who do not belong to club.

We have made a little progress and, perhaps, we have begun to swim with the stream. But, we still have a long way to go.

NOTES TO CHAPTERS

Chapter 2: A quick dip into the history of swimming

1   Both Lencek and Bosker 1998: 38-41 and Sprawson 1992: 67-9 stress the negative effects of the spread of Christianity upon swimming. We know, however, that by the fourteenth and fifteenth centuries people must have been fishing regularly in the sea, since sea fish were consumed in greater quantities than fish from fish ponds, even by households some distance from the sea (Dyer 1988: 30).

2   This paragraph, and the following two, are based on Nicholas Orme's unique account of early British swimming, which includes a reprint of Christopher Middleton's shortened English version of Everard Digby's *De Arte Natandi* together with the illustrations from the original treatise.

3   See Orme 1983: 63 and Vale 1977: 122. Other historians, however, suggest that swimming did not become acceptable for gentlemen until somewhat later, in the early seventeenth century (Gilbert 1954: 12 and Corbin 1994: 5).

4   Sprawson maintains it was confined to a few aristocrats (1992: 70), but Alain Corbin suggests, apparently on the basis of Richard Burton's *Anatomy of Melancholy* which recommends swimming and other outdoor sports as a cure for melancholy, that before about 1620 bathing had been considered an immoral pastime 'better left to the ill-mannered lower classes' (Corbin 1994: 59).

5   Europe experienced a period of cooler weather from the fourteenth to the eighteenth century, which one would expect to have had an influence on the popularity of swimming. Perhaps the increasing popularity of outdoor swimming from the eighteenth century to the mid-twentieth century was, in part, encouraged by warmer weather.

6   Whereas Fox, in his article on the bathing pool at Christ's college, dates its construction as not later the 1650s (Fox 1937), the Royal Commission on Historic Monuments suggests between 1688 and 1746 (RCHM 1959).

7   This information from the Ruislip Lido website: http://www.ruislip.co.uk (March 2004). For more information on lidos generally, see Oliver Merrington's informative website:
http://homepage.ntlworld.com/oliver.merrington/lidos/lidos1.htm.

8   Information from the Amateur Swimming Association's website: www.british-swimming.org (14 February 2004).

9   Charlie Driver's great-granddaughter, Clare O'Reilly, still has the purse and the
     accompanying certificate, but not the gold; conversation with Clare O'Reilly
     (July 2004). See also *Waterlog* for a lively account of swimming in the Cam
     (Deakin 2000).

Chapter 3: Lost opportunities and continuing constraints

1   Rob's Directory is continually updated. See www.Wild-Swimming.com for the
     latest edition.
2   The law relating to towpaths is complex. There are established rights of way
     over some towpaths including much of those alongside the navigable Thames.
     There is no common law right for the public to use towpaths along British
     Waterways canals, but rights have been established alongside many canals.
     Elsewhere towpaths are generally in private ownership (Parker and Penning-
     Rowsell 1980: 165).
3   Michael Dower's seminal article 'The Fourth Wave', published in 1965, is
     frequently cited as a potent influence here. Dower warned that increases in
     population, incomes, mobility, education, retirement and free time threatened
     to overwhelm the countryside, particularly the farmed countryside, unless it
     was planned wisely. He did recognise, however, that the demand for all kinds
     of water sports, including swimming; the reprint of his article in the
     Architect's Journal shows a photo of bank holiday crowds paddling and bathing
     in the Thames at Runnymede.
4   A more important constraint for some people, who may have grown up in
     towns or even in a different country, is not knowing what rights they have
     (University of Brighton 2002: 2.6.1) or lacking the confidence to exercise those
     rights (Countryside Commission 1991a: 10). In recent years many county
     councils, with limited funds for countryside work, have tried to address this
     problem by publishing leaflets and waymarking local walks using existing
     public rights of way.
5   Research in the 1960s indicated that in Britain the favourite landscape was 'a
     calm and peaceful deer park, with slow-moving streams and wide expanse of
     meadowland studded with fine trees' (Lowenthal and Prince 1965:192). A more
     recent survey by MORI for the National Trust found that about half (51 per
     cent) of respondents said that they most value being able to visit the country-
     side near to their homes, areas that they can enjoy all the time, rather than
     more spectacular landscapes further away (MORI 2004).
6   I am grateful to Yakov Lev for guidance on this obscure and uncertain area of
     law.
7   One proposed amendment to the Countryside and Rights of Way Bill sought,
     unsuccessfully, to exclude even streams within the access lands. This would
     have meant that walkers could not legally cross them to continue their walk
     (House of Commons Official Report 1999 – 2000, II: 40). Another amendment
     to extend a 'right to swim' to waters within access lands was opposed in the

House of Lords on conservation grounds (Hansard, 3 October 2000, 616: col.1388).

Chapter 4: The guardians of the water environment

1   The Environment Agency, established under the Environment Act 1995, took up its duties in April 1996 which included, *inter alia*, the functions of the former National Rivers Authority, Her Majesty's Inspectorate of Pollution and the Waste Regulation Authorities. The agency's general duties in relation to recreation come under section 6 (1) of the act, and its specific duties in relation to fisheries under section 6 (6). The special status for fisheries, however, has been long-established, since a Board of Fisheries was set up following the Salmon and Fisheries Act of 1861.

2   The navigation budget goes to improving and maintaining nearly 500 miles of navigable waterways and facilities for commercial and recreational boats, but the volume of freight traffic is very small. A breakdown of the expenditure and income between leisure and freight was unavailable (Email from Naresh Rao, Environment Agency, July 2004). The Corporate Plan 2009-2012 shows an increased emphasis on navigation.

3   Email from Amanda Strang, British Waterways (21 May 2004).

4   The quality of water in canals can vary considerable (Fewtrell *et al* 1993: fig 6.4) but tends to be slightly better than in rivers (Godfree 1993: 150). The British Waterways Water Quality Status Report 1999/2000 indicated that, of their waterways in England and Wales, 68 per cent were classified (under the Environment Agency's classification) as grade D or better in 1992, and this had risen to more than 77 per cent in 1998. By 1998 nearly one-fifth of canals in England and Wales were judged to be of good quality (grades A or B).

5   The Water Resources Act 1963, Section 80, permitted reservoirs to be used by members of the public for any form of recreation considered appropriate.

6   Email from Ian Drury, Public Relations Officer, Wessex Water (26 March 2004).

7   The note stated that:
'(i) the making of bye-laws under section 231 of the Public Health Act 1936 regulating, inter alia, the areas in which, and the hours during which, public bathing is permitted;
(ii) the provision of bathing huts, life belts, or a lifeguard service;
(iii) charging for admission to any bathing place;
(iv) artificially created pools on foreshores (i.e. tanks of concrete or metal which are filled by the incoming tide and subsequently used for bathing.) 'do not amount to explicit authorisation.' (DOE 1980: appendix).

8   The note also stated that a large number of bathers meant: 'it had been assessed that at some time during the bathing season there were at least 500 people in the water (regardless of the length of the stretch of water in question). Any stretch where the number of bathers has been assessed as more that 1500 per mile will be classified as bathing water. Where the number ... [is] ...

between 750 and 1500 per mile water authorities and district councils should discuss whether the water in question is sufficiently well used to be classified ...' (DOE 1980: appendix).

9   Email from Stuart Gibbons, Water Quality Division, DEFRA (18 June 2003).

10   See http://archive.defra.gov.uk/environment/quality/water/pdf/bathing-designation-process.pdf

Chapter 5: A countryside for all?

1   The Countryside Commission, set up after the 1968 Countryside Act with responsibilities for recreation and access to the countryside (but not nature conservation) in England and Wales, was split in 1991 into the Countryside Commission, with a similar remit for England, and the Countryside Council for Wales, with a remit for recreation and nature. The Countryside Agency was established in 1999 by merging the Countryside Commission with parts of the Rural Development Commission, with a remit confined to rural England. English Nature then took over the Countryside Agency's role, together with most of DEFRA's rural development service, in 2005.

2   I have been unsuccessful in finding any reference to a general policy on swimming or a statement from the Forestry Commission.

3   Telephone conversation with Gareth Jones, Forestry Commission (24 March 2003).

4   Information from John Ablitt, Snowdonia National Park Authority (October 2004) and http://snowdonia-active.com/news.asp? (March 2012).

5   Recent research by MORI for the National Trust found that the majority of people (80 per cent of respondents) surveyed think it is important to be able to visit the countryside, and the most important reason they give for doing so is 'peace and quiet'(MORI 2004).

6   Email from Crispin Scott and Hugo Blomfield of the National Trust (October 2003).

7   Email from John Davies, Broads Authority (19 January 2004).

8   Letter from Roger Cole, Operations Manager, Lee Valley Regional Park (19 February 2002).

9   Email from Stewart Pomeroy, Colne Valley Team Manager (March 2012).

10   I am grateful to Liz Waters for giving me access to data from the preliminary returns of the survey carried out by the Urban Parks Forum for the Countryside Commission.

11   Emails from Paul Bolton, Whitlingham Charitable Trust (July 2004) and Lucy Burchnall, Broads Authority (April 2012).

12   Emails from Michelle Little, Free Black Park Campaign (November, 2003).

13   Letter from Sally Silk, Country Park Visitor Manager, Kingsbury Water Park (30 April 2002).

14   Press release by Buckinghamshire County Council (23 April 2002).

Chapter 6: Litigation or liberty?

1   Advice on the River and Lake Swimming Association's website: www.river-swimming.co.uk/hse.htm (July 2003).

2   See note 1.

3   Email from Steve Poolman, HM Inspector of Health and Safety (12 September 2003).

4   An HSE spokesperson explained that it is up to the authority to decide whether or not to accept the executive's advice, but in her experience 'the greatest influence on landowners is their desire to manage the civil litigation risk – this is usually a far more powerful driver than anything HSE has to say' (email from Suzanne Denness, HSE, 1 July 2004).

5   See note 3. Steve Poolman confirmed that HSE had advised Buckinghamshire County Council that 'the risks from allowing (or encouraging) swimming in a relatively uncontrolled environment (specifically without lifeguards) are unacceptably high'.

6   See note 1.

7   The Hon. Michael J. Beloff QC and Javan Herberg, *In the Matter of a Proposal for Self-Regulated Swimming in the Hampstead Ponds,* joint advice addressed to the United Swimmers' Association of Hampstead Heath, October 2003.

8   News release by the Corporation of London, *Self Regulated Swimming – QC's Opinion,* 14 July 2004

Chapter 7: The cost of a quick dip – the danger of drowning

1   The National Water Safety Forum now runs a joint reporting system using information from RoSPA, RLSS, Maritime and Coastguard Agency, Royal Life Saving Society, and others.

2   The foreword to the 2003 edition does not repeat this misleading statement (HSE/Sport England 2003).

3   Lord Hoffman in the House of Lords Judgement in *Tomlinson v. Congleton Borough Council* (2003):para. 39. This was repeated in the *Times* report of the case on 1 August 2003.

4   From 1983 to 1997 RoSPA's statistics were based entirely on local press reports. From 1998 these data were combined with police reports collected by the Home Office, and thus give a more comprehensive picture.

5   Telephone conversation with Peter Cornall, Head of Leisure and Water Safety at RoSPA (September 2002) and email (15 April 2004).

6   Sport England's figures for 1999 indicated that in England swimming is the most popular sport for girls and the third most popular for boys; 50 per cent of young people aged 6 to 16 swim in their spare time. Participation in fishing and other water sports was not high enough to appear in this table (ONS 2002(b): table 13.10).

7   Reported on http//www.ncdc.gov.uk (Sept 2004).

Chapter 8: The cost of a quick dip – the health hazards

1   See www.nhs.uk/conditions/Leptospirosis/Pages/Introduction.aspx (18 May 2009).

2   Dr Robert Smith, who analyses infections for the Health Protection Agency, in the *London Evening Standard* (27 October 2010).

3   See NOIDS Midi Report for 2003, Table 1, published on the web for HPA Communicable Disease Surveillance Centre: www.hpa.org.uk October 2004.

4   Discussion with Mark Thompson, Bristol Henleaze Swimming Club (25 September 2003).

5   Email from David Hoar (2 April 2004) and conversation with Bob Sharman (21 September 2004), both of Swindon Borough Council.

6   Coagulants help to remove dissolved, colloidal or suspended materials by causing them to clump together so that they can be trapped in a filter. This is important in removing *cryptosporidium* and *giardia*, and also humic acid, which is a precursor of THMs (PWTAG 1999: 75).

7   See http://www.defra.gov.uk/statistics/environment/inland-water/iwfg08-biorivqual (March 2012).

Chapter 9: Who wants to swim?

1   Watersports and Leisure Omnibus Surveys www.the-mia.com/assets/Watersports_and_Leisureibusreport2010

2   The Amateur Swimming Association sets the rules for competitive swimming, diving, and water polo matches, but does not encourage unsupervised open-water swimming.

3   These critics include Patmore 1983, Glyptis 1991, Harrison 1991 and Curry 1993 and 1995.

4   Full details of Jonathan Guest's critique were available on www.hatchmere.com/Guest0301.htm (January 2003).

5   Membership of RALSA is free and your support would be welcome: see www.river-swimming.co.uk.

Chapter 10: To cool in the dog days – health and happiness

1   This quotation comes from a letter written in 1700, reproduced in Floyer and Baynard (1722: 31). Floyer was mainly talking about cold baths, rather than swimming, which he recommended as a cure for a wide variety of complaints.

2   The winter swimmers were found to have 'higher initial reduced glutathione concentration and superoxide dismutase and catalase activities in the erythrocytes' than the control group (Siems *et al.*1999: 196).

3   The consultation paper that preceded the 'right to roam' legislation proclaimed that walking in fine countryside could improve our health and refresh our spirits and should be enjoyed by the many rather than the few (DETR 1998: para. 3.66-3.67).

4   It is clear that attitudes to landscapes and wild places are cultural constructs which may change over time. The rugged mountainous areas of the American West, which were home to the native Americans and their source of sustenance, were seen as hostile and threatening by the early settlers. In the mid- and late nineteenth century these same areas became valued as an antidote to urban life, offering their descendants recreational and psychological benefits.

Chapter 11: Tread lightly, swim gently – swimming and the environment

1   Fish graze on *daphnia,* which help to keep the water free from some algae, though not necessarily blue-green algae. Experiments in removing fish from shallow lakes in the Broads have demonstrated how this allows light to penetrate which encourages plant growth (Phillips 1992, Moss 2001).

2   Henleaze Angling Club's rules require that all fishing is done with rod and line, without barbed hooks or live bait. Fish must be handled with care and returned immediately and alive to the water. Keep nets may not be used from April to September, and no fish over 2 lbs may be kept in a keep net at any time.

3   The researchers admitted that in costing the effects of eutrophication on recreational interests they had to use data from other countries.

Chapter 12: Let's swim – making it possible

1   In America, where the state parks and recreation areas commonly provide for swimming, manuals on park management give guidance on selecting and adapting suitable sites for swimming suggesting, for example, that they should be free from pollution and other hazards such as strong currents, that approximately 75 per cent of the designated swimming area should be relatively shallow, 1.5 metres or less, and that disabled access should be provided to the water's edge with a rubber mat on the sand (Sharpe *et al*: 128).

2   Information from Derek Klemperer and Mark Thompson, Henleaze Swimming Club, and Steve Webster, Waverley Borough Council.

3   See www.environment-agency.gov.uk/static/documents/bwprofiles/BW_45650_Windermere_Millerground_Landing.pdf

4   Email from Simon Tilley, Hockerton Housing Project (November 2003) and see also www.hockertonhousingproject.org.uk (March 2012).

5   Discussion with Michael Huntington, South Cambridgeshire District Council (4 July 2001).

6   Information from www.bcu.org.uk (April 2004).

7   The RiverCare Project helps volunteers to look after riversides by providing equipment, insurance cover, advice and information (www.rivercare.org.uk).

8   Email from Elizabeth Kendrick, Friends of the River Shep (January 2004).

9   Telephone conversation with Peter Cornall, RoSPA (September 2002).

10   Telephone conversation with Yacov Lev (August 2003).

11   Email from Steven Miller, Qualifications and Curriculum Authority (June 2004).
12   Research indicates that many people are concerned about very low levels of risk to which they are exposed involuntarily, and prepared to accept far higher levels of risk to do the things that they enjoy (see, for example, Soby and Ball 1991: 21).

Postscript to the second edition

1   Letter from William Crookshank to Yakov Lev (17 July 2008).
2   Email from Tony Stammers, British Waterways to Robert Asprey, Outdoor Swimming Society (16 January 2012).
3   See www.ccw.gov.uk and www.snh.org.uk
4   See www.ccw.gov.uk/about-ccw/consultations/activity-codes-of-conduct.aspx
5   See www.vscg.org.uk/case-studies.
6   Press release 21 March 2009 www.blueprintforwater.org.uk
7   Email from Douglas Caffyn (January 2012)
8   See www.assemblywales.org/newhome/new-news-third-assembly.htm?act=dis&id=125019&ds=5/2009
9   *Hansard*, House of Commons, 13 June 2011, Col. 551W.

REFERENCES

Abbott, C. C. (ed.) 1956 *Further Letters of Gerard Manley Hopkins*, (2nd edition) London: Oxford University Press

Abercrombie, P. 1945 *Greater London Plan 1944*, London: HMSO

Andrews, J. and Kinsman, D. n.d. *Gravel Pit Restoration for Wildlife: A Practical Manual*, Sandy: RSPB

Armstrong, B. and Strachan, D. 2004 'Asthma and swimming pools: statistical issues', *Journal of Occupational and Environmental Medicine* 61: 475-476

Association of Swimming Therapy 1992 *Swimming for People with Disabilities*, London: Black

Aston, M. (ed.) 1988 *Medieval Fish, Fisheries and Fishponds in England*, Oxford: BAR

Atkinson, K. 1995 *Behind the Scenes at the Museum*, London: Transworld Publishers

Ball, D. 1998 'Leisure walking and health', *Countryside Recreation* 6, 2: 4-6

Bates, J. H. 1990 *Water and Drainage Law*, Vol 1, London: Sweet and Maxwell

Bayley, J. 1998 *Iris: A Memoir of Iris Murdoch*, London: Abacus

Baylis, J. *et al* 1995 *Safety and Risk in the Countryside*, Nottingham: East Midlands Council for Sport and Recreation

Bentley, J. 2001 'Countryside access: strategic planning, co-ordination and agri-environmental schemes', *Countryside Recreation* 9, 2: 8-13

Bernard, A. *et al.* 2003 'Lung hypermeability and asthma prevalence in school children: unexpected associations with attendance at indoor chlorinated swimming pools', *Journal of Occupational and Environmental Medicine* 60, 6: 385-394

Biddle, S. and Mutrie, N. 1999 *Psychology of Physical Activity and Exercise: A Health-related Perspective*, London: Springer-Verlag

Blythe, R. 1969 *Akenfield: Portrait of an English Village*, London: Allen Lane

Boorman, J. 2002 *Adventures of a Suburban Boy*, London: Faber

Brailsford, D. *Sport, Time, and Society: The British at Play*, London: Routledge

Branche, C. M., Sniezek, J. E., Sattin, R. W. and Mirkin, I. R. 1991 'Water recreation related spinal injuries: risk factors in natural bodies of water', *Accident Analysis and Prevention* 23, 1: 13-17

British Marine Federation et al. 2009 *Watersports and Participation Survey*, available from www.dft.gov.uk

British Travel Association – University of Keele 1967 *Pilot National Recreation Survey – Report No.1*

British Waterways 2004 (a) *Annual Report and Accounts*, Available online as a pdf file: www.britishwaterways.co.uk/tcm6-85426 (July 2004)

—2004 (b) *Final Accounts*, Available online as a pdf file: www.britishwaterways.co.uk/tcm6-85427.pdf (July 2004)

Broads Authority 1987 *Broads Plan*, Norwich: Broads Authority

Brockway, F. 1977 *Towards Tomorrow: The Autobiography of Fenner Brockway*, London: Hart-Davies

Burnside, J. 2002 'Heat wave' and 'History' in *The Light Trap*, London: Jonathan Cape

Caffyn, D. 2004 *The Right of Navigation on Non-Tidal Waters*, see www.caffynon-rivers.co.uk

Cartright, R 1992 'Recreational waters: a health risk?', in D. Kay (ed.) *op.cit.*

Chu, H. and Nieuwenhuijsen, M. J. 2002 'Distribution and determinants of trihalomethane concentrations in indoor swimming pools', *Journal of Occupational and Environmental Medicine* 59: 243-247

Collinge, R. 1993 'The environmental health constraints' in D. Kay and R. Hanbury (eds.) *op.cit.*

Commission of the European Communities 2000 (a) *Bathing water report*, May 2000

—2000 (b) *Developing a New Bathing Water Policy: Communication from the Commission to the European Parliament and the Council*, Brussels COM (2000) 860 final

Conradi, P. J. 2001 *Iris Murdoch: A Life*, London: Harper Collins

Cooper, C. H. 1843 *Annals of Cambridge, Volume 2*, Cambridge: Warwick and Co.

Cooper, W. Heaton 1983 *The Tarns of Lakeland*, (3rd edition) Kendal: Frank Peters Publishing

Corbin A. 1994 *The Lure of the Sea: The Discovery of the Seaside in the Western World*, (English translation by J. Phelps) Cambridge: Polity Press

Countryside Agency 2002 *State of the Countryside 2002*, Cheltenham: CA

—2003 *Towards a Country Parks Renaissance, Report prepared for the Countryside Agency by the Urban Parks Forum and the Garden History Society*, Cheltenham: CA. Available from www.countryside.gov.uk (November 2003)

Countryside Agency et al. 1999 1998 UK Day Visits Survey, Cheltenham: CA

Countryside Commission 1972 *Policy on Country Parks and Picnic Sites*, Cheltenham: CC

—1989 (a) *Policies for Enjoying the Countryside*, Cheltenham: CC

—1989 (b) *Enjoying the Countryside: Priorities for Action*, Cheltenham: CC

—1991 (a) *Visitors to the Countryside: Consultation Paper*, Cheltenham: CC

—1991 (b) *Caring for the Countryside: A Policy Agenda for England in the Nineties*, Cheltenham: CC

Cousins, S. O' B. and Horne, T. (eds.) 1999 *Active Living among Older Adults: Health Benefits and Outcomes*, Philadelphia: Brunner/Mazel

Curry, N. 1994 *Countryside Recreation, Access and Land Use Planning*, London: Spon

Darby v. National Trust [2001] PIQR 372

Deakin, R. 2000 *Waterlog,* London: Vintage

Department of Health 2004 *At Least Five a Week: Evidence on the Impact of Physical Activity and its Relationship to Health. A Report by the Chief Medical Officer,* London: Department   of   Health   Available   on   line: www.dh.gov.uk/assetRoot/04/08/09/81/04080981.pdh April 2004

Department of the Environment 1980 *Advice Note on the Implementation in England and Wales of the EEC Directive on the Quality of Bathing Water,* (Unpublished)

Department of the Environment, Food and Rural Affairs 2002 *The Environment in Your Pocket: 2002,* London: DEFRA

Department of the Environment, Transport and the Regions 1998 *Access to the Open Countryside in England and Wales: Consultation Paper,* London: HMSO

—2000 (a) *Code of Practice on Conservation, Access and Recreation: Guidance for the Environment Agency and Water and Sewerage Undertakers,* London: HMSO

—2000 (b) *Our Countryside: The Future – A Fair Deal for Rural England,* London: HMSO

Dower, M. 1965 *Fourth Wave: The Challenge of Leisure,* A Civic Trust Survey reprinted from the Architect's Journal, 20 January 1965

Dyckhoff, T 2003 *It's Summer: Take Me to Your Lido,* The Times T2 5 August 2003:16-17

Dyer, C. 1988 'The consumption of freshwater fish in medieval England' in M. Aston (ed.) *op. cit.*

Eastern Council for Sport and Recreation 1989 *Sport in the East: A Strategy for the Nineties. Zone 1 – the Great Ouse and its Associated Waterways*

Eliot, G. 1860 *The Mill on the Floss,* Edinburgh: Blackwood

Ellison, P. and Howe, P. 1997 *Talk of the Wash House,* Liverpool: Picton Press

Emery, J. 1991 *Rose Macaulay: A Writer's Life,* London: John Murray

English Nature 1998 *Access to the Open Countryside in England and Wales: A DETR Consultation Paper. A Response by English Nature,* Peterborough: English Nature

Environment Agency 2001 *State of the Environment Report for London 2001,* Reading: EA

—2004 *Your Rivers for Life Strategy,* Available on line www.environment-agency.gov.uk (January 2004)

—n.d. (a) *An Environmental Vision: The Environment Agency's Contribution to Sustainable Development,* Bristol: Environment Agency

—n.d. (b) *Corporate Plan 2003-06: Priorities, Targets and Planned Use of Resources*

Fewtrell, L. and Jones, F. 1992 'Microbiological aspects and possible health risks of recreational water pollution' in D. Kay (ed.) *op.cit.*

Fewtrell, L., Godfree, A., Jones, F. Kay, D. and Merrett, H. 1994 *Pathogenic Microorganisms in Temperate Environmental Waters,* Cardigan: Samara Publishing Ltd

Finger, M. 1994 'From knowledge to action? Exploring the relationship between environmental experiences, learning, and behaviour', *Journal of Social Issues* 50, 3: 141-160

Floyer, J. and Baynard, E. 1722 *The History of Cold Bathing*, London

Forster, E. M. 1909 *A Room with a View*, London: Edward Arnold

—1960 *The Longest Journey*, (Preface to the 1960 edition) London: OUP

Fox, C. 1937 'The college bathing pool' *Christ's College Magazine* XLIII, 139

Freeman, J. 1997 'A good day' in *The Light is of Love, I Think*, Exeter: Stride

Freeman, R. 1980 *Swimming 1949*, Sycamore Broadsheet 29, Oxford: Sycamore Press

Frumkin, H. 2001 'Beyond toxicity: human health and the natural environment', *American Journal of Preventative Medicine* 20, 3: 47-53

Fryer, R. 2009 *Rob's Directory of Cool Places*, latest edition published as *Rob Fryer's Wild Swimming Guide 2012/13* available from www.Wild-Swimming.com

Gabrielson, M. A. McElhaney, J. and O'Brien, R. 2001 *Diving Injuries: Research Findings and Recommendations for Reducing Catastrophic Injuries,* Boca Raton: CRC Press

Gardner, W. H. 1953 (ed.) *Poems and Prose by Gerard Manley Hopkins,* London: Penguin

Gedge, P. 1947 *Thames Journey: A Book for Boat-Campers and Lovers of the River,* London: Harrap

Gifford, R. 1995 'Natural psychology: an introduction', *Journal of Environmental Psychology* 15: 167-8

Gilbert, E.W. 1954 *Brighton, Old Ocean's Bauble,* London: Methuen

Glyptis, S. 1991 *Countryside Recreation,* Harlow: Longman

Godfree, A. 1993 'Sources and fate of microbial contaminants' in D. Kay and D. Hanbury (eds.) *op. cit.*

Godwin, H. 1978 *Fenland: Its Ancient Past and Uncertain Future*, Cambridge: CUP

Grantham, R. 1993 'Definition of recreational water quality standards in freshwater' in D. Kay and R. Hanbury (eds.) *op. cit.*

Greenhalgh, L. and Worpole, K. 1996 *People, Parks and Cities: A guide to Current Good Practice in Urban Parks,* London: DOE

Griffin, H. 1974 *Long Days in the Hills,* London: Robert Hale

Hampstead Heath Winter Swimming Club v. Corporation of London [2005] EWHC 713 (Admin)

Hankinson, A. 1995 *Geoffrey Winthrop Young: Poet, Educator, Mountaineer,* London: Hodder and Stoughton

Harper, D. M. and Ferguson, A. J. D. (eds.) *The Ecological Basis for River Management,* Wiley: Chichester

Harrison, C. 1991 *Countryside Recreation in a Changing Society*, London: TMS Partnership

Hawkins, T. D. 2000 *The Drainage of Wilbraham, Fulbourn and Teversham Fens,* Little Wilbraham: T. D. Hawkins

Health and Safety Executive/Sport England 1999 *Managing Health and Safety in Swimming Pools HSG 179,* London: HMSO

—2003 *Managing Health and Safety in Swimming Pools HSG 179,* London: HMSO

Hedges, S. G. 1950 *The Complete Swimmer,* London: Methuen

Herbert, A. P. 1969 *Mild and Bitter,* London: Methuen

Hern, A. 1967 *The Seaside Holiday: The History of the English Seaside Resort,* London: Cresset Press

Herzog, T. Chen, H. and Primeau, J. S. 2002 'Perception of the restorative potential of natural and other settings', *Journal of Environmental Psychology* 22: 295-306

Hey, R. D. 1996 'Environmentally sensitive river engineering' in G. Petts and P. Calow (eds.) *op.cit.*

HMSO 1990 *Pollution of Beaches,* House of Commons Environment Committee: fourth report, Volume I-III London: HMSO

House of Commons Official Report 1999 – 2000 *Parliamentary Debates: Session 1999 – 2000*

Hudson, W. 1909 *Afoot in England,* London: Hutchinson

Huxley, E. J. G. 1973 *The Kingsleys: A Biographical Anthology,* London: Allen and Unwin

Ingman, D. 1993 'Opening keynote address' in D. Kay and R. Hanbury (eds.) *op. cit.*

Jackson, L. 2002 'Water wonders' *Guardian Society,* 16 January 2002

Jeal, T. 2004 *Swimming with my Father: A Memoir,* London: Faber

Jefferies, R. 1930 *Bevis,* (Introduction to 1930 edition by Guy Pollock) London: Dent and Sons

Johnson, J. 2004 'Our president writes' in *Conserving Lakeland 24,* Summer/Autumn 2004

Jones, F. 1991 'Public health aspects of the water cycle: a review', in *Applied Geography* 11: 179-186

—1993 'Water industry perspectives: the history of an issue' in D. Kay and R. Hanbury (eds.) *op. cit.*

Kals, F., Schumacher, D. and Montada, L. 1999 'Emotional affinity towards nature as a motivation basis to protect nature', *Environment and Behaviour* 31: 178-202

Kaplan, S. 1995 'The restorative benefits of nature: towards an integrative framework', *Journal of Environmental Psychology* 15: 169-182

Kay, D. (ed.) 1992 *Recreational Water Quality Management, Volume 1: Coastal Waters,* New York: Ellis Horwood

Kay, D. and Hanbury, R. (eds.) 1993 *Recreational Water Quality Management, Volume 2: Fresh Waters,* New York: Ellis Horwood

Kay, D. and Wyer, M. 1992 'Recent epidemiological research leading to standards' in D. Kay (ed.) *op. cit.*

Keynes, G. (ed.) 1967 *Poetry and Prose of William Blake,* London: The Nonesuch Library

Kingsley, C. 1873 *Prose Idylls,* London: Macmillan

Langford, T. and Hill, C. 1992 *Dying of Thirst,* Lincoln: Royal Society for Nature Conservation

Large, A. R. G. and Petts, G. E. 1996 'Rehabilitation of river margins' in G. E. Petts and P. Calow *op. cit.*

Layard, R. 2005 *Happiness: Lessons from a New Science,* London: Allen Lane

Lencek, L. and Bosker, G. 1998 *The Beach: The History of Paradise on Earth,* London: Seckar and Warburg

Liddle, M. 1997 *Recreation Ecology: The Ecological Impact of Outdoor Recreation and Tourism*, London: Chapman & Hall

Lowenthal, D. and Prince, H. C. 1965 'English landscape tastes', *Geographical Review* 55, 2

Macaulay, R. 1968 *Personal Pleasures,* (First published 1935) London: Gollancz

Maitland, P. S. 1995 'Ecological impact of angling', in D. M. Harper and A. J. D. Ferguson (eds.) *op. cit*

—2000 *Guide to Freshwater Fish of Britain and Europe,* London: Hamlyn

Maitland, P. S. and Morgan N. C. 1997 *Conservation Management of Freshwater Habitats: Lakes, River and Wetlands,* London: Chapman & Hall

Manning-Sanders, R. 1951 *Seaside England,* London: Batsford

Moore, G. 1980 *The Lake,* (First published 1905) Gerrards Cross: Colin Smythe

MORI 2004 *Landscapes in Britain: Research Conducted for the National Trust, January 2004*

Morris, W. 1970 *News from Nowhere,* (First published 1890) London: Routledge

Moss, B. 2001 *The Broads: The People's Wetland,* London: Harper Collins

Murdoch, I. 1980 *Nuns and Soldiers,* London: Chatto and Windus

Murdoch, I. 1984 *The Bell,* London: Chatto and Windus

Murphy, K. J., Willby, N. J., and Eaton, J. W. 1995 'Ecological impacts and management of boat traffic on navigable inland waterways' in D. M. Harper and A. J. D. Ferguson (eds.) *op. cit.*

National Rivers Authority 1990 *Toxic Blue-Green Algae,* Water Quality Series No.2. September 1990 London: NRA

Office of National Statistics 1998 *Living in Britain: Results from the 1996 General Household Survey* London: HMSO

—2004 *Sport and Leisure: Results from the Sport and Leisure Module of the 2002 General Household Survey,* London: TSO

Orme, N. 1983 *Early British Swimming 55 BC – AD 1719,* Exeter: University of Exeter Press

Overhill, J. 1945 *Swimming for Fun,* Second draft of an unpublished memoir

Packman, R. 1993 'Summary and observations' in D. Kay and R. Hanbury, (eds.) *op. cit.*

Palmer, J. A. 1998 'Spiritual ideas, environmental concerns and educational practice' in D. E. Cooper and J. A. Palmer (eds.) *Spirit of the Environment: Religion, Value and Environmental Concern,* London: Routledge

Parker, D. J. and Penning-Rowsell, E. C. 1980 *Water Planning in Britain*, London: Allen and Unwin

Parker, R. 1977 *The Common Stream*, St Albans: Palladin

Pearce, P 1978 *The Minnow on the Say*, (First published 1955) London: Puffin Books

Pears, T. 1993 *In the Place of Fallen Leaves*, London: Black Swan Books

Penning-Rowsell, E. C., Parker, D. J. and Harding, D. M. 1986 *Floods and Drainage*, London: Allen and Unwin

Petts, G. E. and Calow, P. (eds.) 1996 *River Restoration*, Oxford: Blackwell

Philipp, R. Waitkins, S. Caul, Roome, A. McMahon, S. and Enticott, R. G. 1989 'Leptospiral and Hepatitis A antibodies amongst windsurfers and waterskiers in Bristol City Docks', *Public Health* 103:123-129

Philipp, R., Evans, E. .J., Hughes, A. O., Grisdale, S. K., Enticott, R. G. and Jephcott, A. E. 1985 'Health risks of snorkel swimming in untreated water', *International Journal of Epidemiology* 14: 624-627

Phillips, D. 1997 *The River Nene: From Source to Sea*. Peterborough: Past and Present Publishing

Phillips, G. 1992 'A case study in restoration: shallow eutrophic lakes in the Norfolk Broads' in D. Harper *Eutrophication of Freshwaters: Principles, Problems and Restoration*, London: Chapman Hall

Plomer, W. (ed.) 1969 *Kilvert's Diary: Selections from the Diary of the Rev. Frances Kilvert 23 August 1971 – 13 May 1874, Volume 2*, London: Cape

Pool Water Treatment Advisory Group 1999 *Swimming Pool Water: Treatment and Quality Standards* Diss: PWTAG

Poulsen, C. 1976 *Victoria Park*, London: Journeyman Press

Pretty, J. N., Griffin, M., Sellens, M. and Pretty, C. 2003 *Green Exercise: Complementary Roles of Nature, Exercise and Diet in Physical and Emotional Well-being and Implication for Public Health Policy*, Occasional paper 2003-1 University of Essex Centre for Environment and Society

Pretty, J. N., Mason, C. F., Nedwell, D. B. and Hine, R. E. 2003 'Environmental costs of fresh water eutrophication in England and Wales' *Environmental Science and Technology* 37, 2: 201-208

Provine, R. R. 2000 *Laughter: A Scientific Investigation*, London: Faber

Pruss, A.1998 'Review of epidemiological studies on health effects from exposure to recreational water', *International Journal of Epidemiology* 27: 309-315

Purseglove, J. 1988 *Taming the Flood: A History and Natural History of Rivers and Wetlands*, Oxford: OUP

Purves, L. 2003 'Taking the plunge', *Saga Magazine* April 2003

Randolph, T. 1643 *Randolph's Poems*, London

Ransome, A. 1962 *Swallows and Amazons*, (First published 1930) Harmondsworth: Penguin Books

Raverat, G. 1960 *Period Piece: A Cambridge Childhood*, London: Faber

Read, M. 2000 *Forever England: The Life of Rupert Brooke*, Edinburgh: Mainstream Publishing

Rew, K. 2008 *Wild Swim*, London: Guardian Books

RoSPA 1987 'Drownings in the UK 1986', *Water and Leisure Accident Prevention* Spring 1987

—'Drownings in the UK 1995', *Water and Leisure Accident Prevention* Spring 1995

—*Safety at Inland Water Sites: Operational Guidelines*, Birmingham: RoSPA

—n.d. *Drowning Statistics in the UK 2001*, CDRom Birmingham: RoSPA

Royal Commission on Historical Monuments, England 1959 *City of Cambridge: Part I*, London: HMSO

Royal Life Saving Society UK 1983 *Drownings in the British Isles 1982*

RSPB, NRA and RSNC 1994 *The New Rivers and Wildlife Handbook*, Sandy: RSPB

Sanghera, S. 2004 'I'm 27 and I can't swim: time to take the plunge', *Financial Times* 13 March 2004

Scottish Natural Heritage 2004 Scottish Outdoor Access Code, Edinburgh: SNH

Segrell, B. 1996 'Accessing the attractive coast: conflicts and co-operation in the Swedish coastal landscape during the twentieth century' in C. Watkins (ed.) *Rights of Way: Policy, Culture and Management*, London: Pinter

Sexby, J. J. 1898 *The Municipal Parks, Gardens, and Open Spaces of London: Their History and Associations*, London: Elliot Stock

Sharpe, G. W., Odegaard, C. H. and Sharpe, W. F. 1983 *Park Management*, New York: Wiley

Shephard, R. J. 1997 'What is the optimal type of activity to enhance health?', *British Journal of Sports Medicine* 31: 277-284

Shoard, M. 1979 'Children in the countryside', *The Planner* May 1979: 67-71

—1980 *The Theft of the Countryside*, London: Temple Smith

—1997 *This Land is Our Land: The Struggle for Britain's Countryside*, London: Gaia Books

—1999 *A Right to Roam*, Oxford: OUP

Siems, W. G., Brenke, R., Sommerburg, O. and Grune, T. 1999 'Improved antioxidative protection in winter swimmers', *Quarterly Journal of Medicine* 92: 191-198

Sinclair, G. 1992 *The Lost Land: Land Use Change in England 1945-1990*, London: CPRE

Spalding, F. 2001 *Gwen Raverat: Friends, Family and Affections*, London: Harvill Press

Sport England 2001 *Disability Survey 2000: Young People with a Disability and Sport. Headline Findings*, London: SE

Sports Council 1990 *A Countryside for Sport: Towards A Policy for Sport and Recreation in the Countryside: A Consultation*, London: SC

—1992 *A Countryside for Sport: A Policy for Sport and Recreation*, London: SC

Sprawson, C. 1992 *Haunts of the Black Masseur: The Swimmer as Hero*, Jonathan Cape: London

Stanwell-Smith, R. 'Public health and epidemiological aspects' in D. Kay and R. Hanbury (eds.) *op. cit.*

Start, D. 2008 *Wild Swimming*, London: Punk Publishing

Steane, J. M. 1988 'The royal fishponds of medieval England' in M. Aston (ed.) *op. cit.*

Steensberg, J. 1998 'Epidemiology of accidental drowning in Denmark 1989-1993', *Accident Analysis and Prevention,* 30, 6: 755-762

Steinberg, H., Sykes, E. A., Moss, T., Lowery S., Le Boutillier, N. and Dewey, A. 1997 'Exercise enhances creativity independently of mood', *British Journal of Sports Medicine* 31: 240-45

Swift, J. 1974 *Journal to Stella: Volume I,* (Ed. Harold Williams) Oxford: Blackwell

Taylor, C. C. 1988 'Problems and possibilities' in M. Aston (ed.) *op.cit.*

Tomlinson v Congleton Borough Council [2003] 3 WLR 705 HL(E)

Ulrich, R. S. 1993 'Biophilia, biophobia and natural landscapes' in S. R. Kellert and E. O. Wilson (eds.) *op. cit.*

University of Brighton 2001 *Water-Based Sport and Recreation: The Facts,* School of the Environment, University of Brighton

Vale, M. 1977 *The Gentleman's Recreations: Accomplishments and Pastimes of the English Gentleman 1580-1630,* Cambridge: Brewer

Van Asperen, I. A., Medema, G., Borgdorff, M. W. and Sprenger, M. J. W. 1998 'Risk of gastroenteritis among triathletes in relation to faecal pollution of fresh water', *International Journal of Epidemiology* 27: 309-315

Van Leeuvan, T. A. P. 1998 *The Springboard in the Pond: An Intimate History of the Swimming Pool,* Cambridge MA: MIT Press

White, N. 1992 *Hopkins: A Literary Biography,* Oxford: Clarendon Press

Williams, S. 1995 *Outdoor Recreation and the Urban Environment,* London: Routledge

Williamson, H. 1959 *The Children of Shallowford,* (First published 1939) London: Faber

Wilson, W. 1913 *The New Freedom* (Wilson's speeches ed. W. B. Hale), London: Chapman and Hall

Worpole, K. 2000 *Here Comes the Sun,* London: Reaktion Books

Young, G. W. 1936 *Collected Poems of Geoffrey Winthrop Young,* London: Methuen

INDEX

Abercrombie, Sir Patrick, 43, 48
access to lakes and rivers, 27-31
agricultural changes, 24-5
Amateur Swimming Association, 17, 19, 59, 81, 83, 108, 122, 128
angling, x, xii, 31, 34, 65, 67, 80, 967, 127; *see also* drowning
Asprey, Robert, 119
Atkinson, Kate, 7
attitudes to swimming, in literature, 1-11; in public policy, 35-49

bans on inland swimming, xiv, 37-8, 50-1, 57, 59, 73, 84-6
barley straw, 73-5, 106; *see also* blue-green algae
Bathing Water Directive, 27, 33, 35-6, 39, 77, 84, 86, 106
Bedford River Valley Park, 119
Benyon, Richard, 122
Black Park Country Park, 50-1, 84
blue book, 55, 60, 118; *see also* Health and Safety Executive
blue-green algae, control of, 75, 99, 106; hazards of, 74-5, 78; incidence of, 26, 47, 71, 73-4, 105; use as a threat, 57, 105
Blueprint for Water, 121
Boorman, John 3, 7
Brereton Country Park, 50, 57, 121
British Canoe Union, 31, 67, 108, 122
British Waterways, xv, 33, 36-7, 53-4
Broads, the, 47, 49, 81
Bude Pool, 19, 69
Burnside, John, 5
by-laws, 27, 33, 37, 45-8, 120

Byron's Pool, xiv, 27, 120

Caffyn, Douglas, xii, 30, 122
Cam Conservators, 119
Cam, river, xiv, 8, 10, 12-3, 16, 20-1, 23, 27
Canal and River Trust, 36, 119
canals, 36-7, 124; *see also* drownings
canoeing, 35, 38, 45, 71, 116; *see also* drownings
Cheshire Fire Service, 120
children, safety of 110,114-5; *see also* drownings
chlorine compounds, 75-6
Coate Water, 70, 73-4
cold water, effects on body, *see* health benefits, health hazards
Colne Valley Regional Park, 48-9,
Compton Lock, 113
Cornall, Peter, 110-2, 118
Cotswold Water Park, 41, 49, 51, 105
country parks, 43, 48-52, 103
Countryside Act 1968, 28, 49, 125
Countryside Agency, 29, 43-4, 50, 112, 125
Countryside and Rights of Way (CROW) Act 2000, xii, 28-9, 31, 116
Countryside Commission, 43-4, 49, 50, 79, 126
Countryside Council for Wales, 43-4, 119, 120
Crookshank, William, 118
cryptosporidium, 75
cyanobacterial toxins, *see* blue-green algae

Darby v. National Trust (2001), 57
De Arte Natandi, *see* Digby, Everard
Deakin, Roger, 4, 5, 70, 121
Digby, Everard, 13, 14, 123
Ditchford, xiv, 20, 21
Driver, Charlie, 20, 123
drownings, accidental, 61-9;
  involving alcohol, 62-3; involving
  angling, 62, 67; involving
  canoeing, 62, 67; involving
  children, 63; involving sub aqua,
  62, 67, 127; involving swimming,
  61-3, 67; location of, 64-6
duty of care, 31, 53-55, 58, 116; *see
  also* Occupiers' Liability Acts,
  Health and Safety at Work Act

Ederle, Gertrude, 19
education, outdoor, 114-5
English Nature, 43, 120
enterococci, intestinal, 77
Environment Act 1995, 46, 124
Environment Agency, xv, 33-6, 42,
  53-4, 61, 86, 106, 109, 118, 121
environmental impacts, of angling,
  96-7; of water-based sports, 96; of
  wild swimming, 97
environmental synergies, 98-100
escherischia coli, 77
European Commission, 33, 38-42

faecal coliforms, 70, 77
faecal streptococci, 77
Farleigh Hungerford, 82, 87, 109,
  110
Fens, the, 25, 35
Fire and Rescue Services, 61, 120
fishing, *see* angling
flood control, 99, 100, 108; *see also*
  river engineering
Forestry Commission, 28, 44-7
Forster, E.M., 2, 23
France, 40, 115

Freeman, John, 10-1
Freeman, Richard, 3
Frensham Great Pond, 41, 51, 103-4
Frome, river, 82, 110
Fryer, Rob, 23-4, 29, 79, 114, 118

gastroenteritis, 71, 77
Geirionydd, Llyn, 45-6
General Household Survey, 65, 80
Germany, 40, 90, 107
Great Wilbraham, river, 26
Griffin, Harry, 92

Hampstead Heath ponds, 41, 59, 60,
  86-7, 103
happiness, 1-11, 93-4
Harman, Sir John, 118
Hatchmere Lake, 85, 87, 112
Health and Safety at Work Act 1974,
  55, 58-59, 60
Health and Safety Executive, 52, 55-
  6, 59, 60, 62, 66, 118
health benefits, 88-9; of cold water,
  89, 90, 129; of exercise, 90-1; of
  outdoor exercise, 91-3; of
  swimming, 88-9
health hazards, 70-8, 89
Henleaze Swimming Club and Lake,
  73, 83, 97, 106, 109
Herbert, A. P., 29
history of swimming, 12-22
Hobhouse, Lord, 52, 57, 61
Hockerton Housing Project, 106
Hodder, river, 7, 10
Hoffman, Lord, 58
Hopkins, Gerard Manley, 1, 4, 7, 10

Jefferies, Richard, 73
joys of wild swimming, 1-11, 88

Keynes Country Park, *see* Cotswold
  Country Park
Kilvert, Reverend Francis, 15

Kingsbury Water Park, 52
Kingsley, Charles, 4, 6, 25

Lake District, xiv, 46, 92
lakes, mineral extraction, 48-9, 57,
    83, 103, 105; 'natural' swimming
    ponds, 107-8; water quality, 77,
    103-5; see also reservoirs
land drainage, 24-6,
land managers, 44-52: see also duty
    of care
landowners, attitudes to swimming,
    30-1, 112, 114; rights over water x,
    30; see also duty of care
Land Reform (Scotland) Act 2003, xi,
    xii, 31
landscape, attitudes to, 29, 124
Lechlade, 29, 113
Lee Valley Regional Park, 48-9
leptospiral infections, see Weil's
    disease
Lev, Yakov, 85, 118
lidos, 18-19
litigation, 52-3, 57, 73, 116
local authorities xv, 47-52, 54, 103-5;
    see also country parks, regional
    parks
Lloyd, Val, 121
Luxembourg, 40

Macaulay, Rose, 3, 10, 31
Marine Conservation Society, 40 108
Mersey, river, 17-18, 26
Middleton, Christopher, 13
Milton Pits Country Park, 50
Morris, William, 10
Mungovan, Rob, 119
Murdoch, Iris, 2, 3, 6

national curriculum, see education,
    outdoor
National Parks and Access to the
    Countryside Act 1949, 28

national parks, national park
    authorities, 45-7
National Water Safety Forum, 61, 64
National Trust, 45, 47, 56, 86, 113,
navigation, public expenditure on,
    34, 37, 124; rights of, xii, 30
Nedd, river, 45
Nene, river, xiv, 20
Netherlands, 40, 42
Norway, 117

Occupiers' Liability Acts 1957 and
    1984, 54, 58, 60
Orme, Nicholas, 7, 13-4, 15, 123
Outdoor Swimming Society, 118, 130

participation, in angling, 65, 67, 80,
    127; in canoeing, 65, 67, 127; in
    sub aqua, 67, 127; in swimming,
    65, 80; in windsurfing, 65
Pearce, Philippa, 116

Raverat, Gwen, 1, 2, 8, 9, 31, 87
regional parks, 48-9
reservoirs, 38, 77, 118
right to roam, xii, 92, 116-7, 129; see
    also Countryside and Rights of Way
    Act 2000
right to swim, 30-2, 116, 122; see
    also Countryside and Rights of Way
    Act 2000
risk, attitudes to, 115, 118
risks of swimming, see drownings,
    health hazards
River Access Campaign, 108, 122
River and Lake Swimming
    Association (RALSA), 86, 108, 118
RiverCare Project, 108-9
river engineering, 24, 99, 100, 108
river restoration, 100, 108
Royal Society for the Prevention of
    Accidents (RoSPA), 43, 52-3, 55-6,
    61-9, 119

Ruislip Lido, 18, 122
Rutland Water, 38, 119

sailing, 35, 81
Scottish Natural Heritage, xii, 119
sea bathing, dangers, 64, 67; history
   of, 14-15, 89; *see also* drownings
Serpentine, the, 41
Shoard, Marion, viii, 23, 30, 116
Snowdonia, Snowdonia National
   Park, 45-6,
Sports Council, 44, 112
Sprawson, Charles, 7, 123
Start, Daniel, xiii
sub aqua, 62, 66-8, 75, 77
Surfers against Sewage, 40
sustainable urban drainage systems,
   107-8
Sweden, 42, 117,
swimming baths, *see* swimming
   pools
swimming clubs, 19, 31, 59, 112
swimming pools, drownings in, 62;
   health problems of, 70, 75-6;
   history of, 13, 15-18; management
   guidelines for, *see* blue book

Thames, river, 26-7, 29, 30, 35, 112-3
Thet, river, 27
Tinside Lido, 19
*Tomlinson v. Congleton Borough
   Council* (2003), 53, 57-8, 60-1,
triathlons, 38, 48, 71, 77
trihalomethanes, 76; *see also*
   chlorine compounds

United Swimmers' Association,
   Hampstead Heath, 59, 127
University of Brighton study, x, 27-8,
   30, 81, 108
Urban Parks Forum, 50

Voluntary access agreements, 122

Victoria Park, 16-17, 43

water, abstraction, 25-6, 122;
   pollution, 26-7; quality, 37-42, 76-
   7, 105-6, 124; *see also* lakes,
   blue-green algae
water companies, xv, 28, 33, 38, 54,
   119
Water Framework Directive, 121
water-skiing, 38, 77
Webb, Captain, 19
Weil's disease, 48, 56, 71; incidence
   of, 71-3, 128; threat of, 56-7, 71, 73
Welsh Assembly, 122
Whitlingham Country Park, 50
Whittie, Dr, 14
Whittlesey Mere, 25
Wicken Fen, 25
wildlife conservation, 26, 34, 36, 73,
   85, 99, 100, 102, 105, 107-8, 117
Windermere, Lake, 41, 45-6, 86, 113
women and swimming, 7, 8, 17, 19,
   20
Wordsworth, William, 1, 10
Wye, river (Wales), 30, 35

Young, Geoffrey Winthrop, 6, 9, 10,
   31

Printed and bound by CPI Group (UK) Ltd, Croydon, CR0 4YY